MURDER ABOARD

MURDER ABOARD

The Herbert Fuller *Tragedy and the Ordeal of Thomas Bram*

C. Michael Hiam

Essex, Connecticut

An imprint of Globe Pequot, the trade division of
The Rowman & Littlefield Publishing Group, Inc.
4501 Forbes Blvd., Ste. 200
Lanham, MD 20706
www.rowman.com

Distributed by NATIONAL BOOK NETWORK

British Library Cataloguing in Publication Information available

Library of Congress Cataloging-in-Publication Data available

ISBN 978-1-4930-5945-4 (paperback)
ISBN 978-1-4930-4132-9 (ebook)

∞™ The paper used in this publication meets the minimum requirements of American National Standard for Information Sciences—Permanence of Paper for Printed Library Materials, ANSI/NISO Z39.48-1992.

Some went down to the sea in ships
and plied their trade in great waters;
They beheld the works of the LORD
and his wonders in the deep.
Then he spoke and a stormy wind arose,
which tossed high the waves of the sea.
They mounted up to the heavens and fell back to the depths;
their hearts melted because of their peril.
They reeled and staggered like drunkards
and were at their wits' end.
Then they cried to the LORD in their trouble,
and he delivered them from their distress.
He stilled the storm to a whisper
and quieted the waves of the sea.
Then they were glad because of the calm,
and he brought them to the harbor they were bound for.

Psalm 107: 23–30

CHAPTER 1

On the morning of Friday, July 3, 1896, a steam tug towed the barkentine *Herbert Fuller* from Long Wharf to Boston Harbor's deepwater anchorage at Nantasket Roads. Here the tow ended; the tug departed for other duties, while the *Herbert Fuller*, preferring for now the shelter of neighboring islands to the thick fog and easterly headwind of the Atlantic Ocean beyond, dropped anchor.

Floating up and down to the gentle swell of the roads, the *Herbert Fuller* made for an attractive sight. It was a graceful vessel, with a sharp bow and tapering stern; sleek wooden hull painted black with white trim; and three masts that, for now, were bereft of the billowing sails that would have completed the picture. According to *Lloyd's Register*, the *Herbert Fuller* had been built six years earlier in 1890; weighed 701 gross tons; measured 158 feet in length, 36 feet in breadth, 18 feet in depth; and could be sailed by a crew of eight.

The voyage ahead would be six thousand miles to Buenos Aires and then another two hundred miles up the Paraná River to the city of Rosario. There the *Herbert Fuller*'s cargo of white pine boards was to be discharged. Those boards, comprising 700,000 linear feet and valued at $15,000, took up almost every available inch of the *Herbert Fuller*, occupying all of the 'tween deck and lower hold below, as well as all of the main deck topside, where they were piled five feet high from the afterhouse in the stern to the forward house in the bow.

During the sixty- or seventy-day sail to Argentina, these two houses would serve as living quarters for the eleven men and one woman aboard. Those souls were the captain, his wife, two mates, a steward, six sailors, and a passenger. The latter was Lester Hawthorne Monks, a twenty-year-old student at Harvard University's Lawrence Scientific School.

Monks had inspected the *Herbert Fuller* two weeks prior, June 16, as it lay at Mystic Wharf. The vessel had just left the East Boston dry dock, where its hull had been caulked for leaks, and was now in the process of shifting sixty tons of stone ballast and loading the first of the white pine destined for Argentina.

On that day, Monks would have presented as the well-dressed, soft-spoken, and perfectly mannered college boy that he was, hence making him somewhat out of place onboard a working ship. In fact, the tall but slightly built collegian did not appear the working type at all and, with his pale face, slightly stooped shoulders, and awkward gait, actually looked kind of sickly.

The *Herbert Fuller*'s captain was away at the time, and so it had fallen on the second-in-command, the mate, Thomas Bram, to welcome Monks onboard. In contrast to Monks, Bram was age thirty-three and of muscular build. He stood five feet seven inches tall and had piercing black eyes, soft black hair, and a deep and powerful voice. Also unlike Monks, Bram had darkish skin that made him appear, according to contemporary descriptions, as "almost white" or, alternatively, "nearly negro."

The mate dutifully showed the young man around but frankly advised against taking a sailing vessel for such an extended journey, explaining that, if he were a man of means (as Monks obviously was), he would prefer a large passenger steamer for its greater speed and comfort. The mate added that, from his own experience, there would be more to see and learn onboard a big ship than on a smaller vessel like the *Herbert Fuller*.

Monks, however, replied firmly that he intended to arrive in South America under sail, being perhaps too shy to mention that his uncle, a physician, had strongly recommended an unhurried sojourn at sea. Indeed, Monks suffered from weak lungs, knee problems (as a result of a bicycle accident), and other maladies that had greatly interfered with his studies. After two years in Cambridge, the college boy's grades had been dismal, nearly all Es (an E at Harvard in the 1890s meaning, not "excellent," but one notch above an F), and as the semester just ended, there were no grades at all: The young man had skipped his final exams.

Realizing that time on the ocean would do his son good, Lester's father, Franklin Monks, a man well known in Boston business circles, fully approved of the sailing idea and had made careful inquiries among the city's shipping agents regarding a captain he could entrust with his son's care and safety. From the firm of John P. Ellicott & Co. came the name of a master mariner, Charles I. Nash of the *Herbert Fuller*, who looked to fit the bill.

A superior type of captain and one of the best known to sail from the state of Maine, Nash hailed from Harrington, where his was an old and respected Down East family. His father, Alonso Nash, had been a master mariner and a noted shipowner and builder before being killed in a tragic shipyard accident a few years before. Two of Charles Nash's four brothers had also chosen to follow the sea, and now age forty-two, Nash had captained ships for twenty years and, as Franklin Monks learned to his satisfaction, "knew his business and he attended to it."

What the senior Monks probably didn't know (but would hardly have been upset if he had) was that Nash, who was short in stature but rock hard in muscle, had the physical strength of two ordinary men, plus his revolver, with which to exert his authority if any crew member stepped out of line. And for those who continued to give trouble, Nash, like all captains on the high seas, could have anyone seized and clapped into irons.

A captain's authority did not extend to the natural elements, however, and once during a raging storm, a huge wave had washed Nash and everything else not tied down overboard. Twice the captain had disappeared beneath the boiling waters, but with luck he found some floating spars and clung to these long enough to be rescued by his anxious men.

For the past six years, Nash had been master and part owner of the *Herbert Fuller*, a vessel whose construction in his father's shipyard he had personally supervised, inspecting every inch of timber, iron, and copper that went into it. He had given particular attention to the afterhouse, doing all that he could to make it as comfortable as possible for both himself and his wife, the former Laura A. Ray.

The two had met in Harrington, she sixteen and daughter of a sea captain, and he just twenty but soon to become a sea captain himself. The young mariner courted the maiden on the village sidewalks during his time ashore, and in due course the couple became man and wife. Although never blessed with children, Charles and Laura had each other, and by 1896 the couple had spent all but two of their sixteen years of marriage as seagoing companions. Their voyages had taken them up and down the East Coast, to and from South America, back and forth across the Atlantic, into the Mediterranean, and even to the southern tip of Africa, Cape Town.

Aboard ship, Laura kept to herself, talking only to her husband and if need be to the steward, though she always displayed a quiet kindness toward the other men, ensuring, for example, that they received hot coffee in the coldest weather. For this and for her noble bearing, the sailors thought Laura a splendid woman. While never the subject of scandal, her years at sea had not been without incident.

A memorable one occurred in April 1885 as she accompanied her husband aboard his bark *John F. Rottman* bearing a cargo of sugar from Brazil to Canada. Severe storms had damaged the vessel's hull along the way, requiring that the pumps be manned at all times. Added to this handicap was the fact that deadly fumes coming from the load of sugar sickened all but two of Captain Nash's men. With only these two to help him both work the pumps and sail the vessel, Nash managed to reach Bermuda a fortnight later, by which time four of those taken ill had died. On other, more routine trips, Captain and Mrs. Nash could be seen walking arm in arm around the slanting deck, as placidly as if taking a stroll back in Harrington.

Accompanied by his many belongings and two friends, Lester Monks boarded the *Herbert Fuller* on the night of July 2, the last day the barkentine was at Long Wharf. Having got no sleep in his small cabin, made hot and stuffy by the July heat, at daybreak Monks joined his father and a friend for breakfast ashore. Then it came time to bid his leave, and as the tug eased the *Herbert Fuller* from Long Wharf, the young man had to have wondered when he would see kith and kin again. Almost immediately, it turned out.

The first day of waiting at Nantasket Roads for better weather stretched into a second and then a third day. Monks did a little exercising on deck and was entertained on the night of July Fourth by a cannon salute coming from nearby Fort Warren. Also nearby was the resort town of Hull, and from there the young man's mother, father, sister, uncle, aunt, and assorted friends took a boat ride out to the

Herbert Fuller and said their farewells all over again. Otherwise, Monks was bored and, in the gentle swell of the roads, seasick. Captain Nash advised that they should be able to sail on July 6, but that day came and went with weather conditions unchanged. The following day, July 7, Monks wrote dejectedly in his diary, "Nantasket Roads are very familiar to me, however as a summer resort they are a failure."

Finally on Wednesday morning, July 8, the young man woke to the thrilling sight of the crew raising the mainsail. A fresh breeze had arisen from the west, the fog had lifted, and the *Herbert Fuller* hove anchor for a tow out to the Boston lightship, where at seven thirty it was released into Massachusetts Bay. Nash, who knew these waters well, set a course toward the southern boundary of Georges Bank before setting another course due south around Cape Cod. Monks was finally on his way to South America.

In the 1890s, the sea date began at twelve noon and not twelve midnight, meaning that five hours later it was already Thursday, July 9, the *Herbert Fuller* having placed thirty-five miles between itself and Boston so far. Then twenty-four hours later, the distance increased, according to the ship's log, to 165 miles. On the third day under sail, Boston was recorded as being 326 miles away. Ever since leaving sight of shore, the log noted, no other vessels had been sighted, the seas had varied from calm to moderate, the winds had been from the south and southwest, and the skies were overcast.

Later, none of the *Herbert Fuller*'s survivors could recall anything unusual during this stage of the voyage, with the consensus being that everything seemed "pleasant" and "harmonious" onboard. The passenger certainly noticed nothing out of the ordinary, his brief diary entry for July 11 being typical: "*This is great*, I have lived twenty years but have not seen a day like this. Lost another dolphin this afternoon. Rained all night drops as large as silver dollars. Not much wind however."

By now Monks would have made himself at home in the close confines of the afterhouse, an apartment of eight rooms squeezed into just 470 square feet of floor space. The trapezoidal structure with its flat roof rose five feet above deck level, with another two feet sunk below in the hull, giving it an interior ceiling height of six feet ten inches.

To enter or exit the afterhouse, the captain and his wife had the exclusive use of the four steps of the after companionway leading to and from the stern deck, while the steward and the mates used the four steps of the forward companionway leading to and from the main deck. Because on this voyage the cargo of white pine boards lay flush with the afterhouse roof, four more steps were fashioned from the pine to reach the forward companionway entrance to the top of the deck load. As another measure taken just for this trip, a temporary railing had been constructed along the sides of the deck load to prevent the careless from tumbling into "the brine."

Inside the afterhouse a skylight and a series of small windows along the upper part of the four exterior walls provided light during the day, and at night a swinging lantern illuminated a grandiosely named but tiny area called the main cabin. The main cabin had a small but adequate coal stove, as well as the vessel's only way of telling the time: a clock that hung on a partition next to a handsome table made of thick black walnut. It was at this table where Monks took his midday dinners and evening suppers.

While seated at the table, Monks could have practically touched the doors of the diminutive staterooms belonging to the two mates. The second mate's stateroom, only four feet wide and maybe twice that in length, might be confused for a closet, with the mate's stateroom not much larger. In comparison, Captain and Mrs. Nash occupied a private and attractively decorated domain that took up two-thirds of the afterhouse interior. Within this space the couple had two staterooms, divided by a partition of matched boards with a doorway in the middle. The room Mrs. Nash occupied, the larger of the two, was off the main cabin and had a black walnut bunk the size of a double bed, as well as a closet, a dressing table, a chair, and a large square trunk. According to a newspaper reporter who later toured the afterhouse, a Brussels carpet adorned the floor, the walls were painted white alternating with natural wood, and overall the decor was in the best style.

The captain's stateroom was considerably smaller and lacked a carpet or any furnishings other than a single bunk. However, as the same reporter noted approvingly, "There was nothing about the cabin to jar upon sensitive and cultivated tastes," the woodwork having been "stained a rich cherry, and here and there a conventional design, done in gold and blue, was to be seen."

The captain's stateroom adjoined an aft cabin, which on the *Herbert Fuller* was called the chart room. As the preserve of just the captain and his wife, the chart room was a boudoir for her and a study and library for him. The same reporter observed that it, too, had been done up in style. Another Brussels carpet graced the floor, the walls were painted an immaculate white with touches of gold paint and narrow gilded beading appearing at regular intervals. On the ceiling decorative details had been carved into polished beams of timber.

The chart room also possessed domestic niceties rarely found on a workaday barkentine. These included an upholstered divan, a large fold-out desk, and a little musical organ of the melodeon type. Located in the aft port corner of the afterhouse was a lavatory, also reserved for the exclusive use of the captain and his wife. The lavatory had running cold water, porcelain bowls for washing, and (although the reporter failed to mention this) a wooden seat with a small hole in the middle that led directly to the ocean.

At the dining table in the main cabin of the afterhouse, Monks also sat just feet from the pantry, with its shelves well stocked with plates, cutlery, and glassware, as well as the storeroom, in which was kept the canned meats, vegetables, fruits, and other small stores intended for consumption at the captain's table. When the door of the storeroom was left open, Monks later admitted that he could clearly see an ax on the wall. The ax, meant for emergency purposes such as having to chop down rigging in a storm, was brand new and lightweight. It had a white painted head that was sharp on one end and blunt on the other. Its unpainted wood handle was about two and a half feet long.

One of the few things the afterhouse did not boast were passenger accommodations, and so the two Nashes had graciously welcomed him into their private abode. As their guest, Monks was free to use the chart room, lavatory, and after companionway as if they were his own. In terms of a berth, the smaller stateroom, the one usually occupied by the captain, was given over to him. A displaced Captain Nash slept on a mattress and cot in the chart room.

Monks did not travel light, and the inventory of items he brought aboard included two steamer trunks, a dress suitcase, sixty bottles of beer, books, a bottle of whiskey, a bottle of brandy, some crackers, boxes of cigars, and a cartload of fruit. Those things that didn't fit in his small stateroom had gone into the afterhouse storeroom, but certainly not his six dollars in cash, a letter of credit for five hundred pounds of sterling, a letter of introduction to prominent people in South America, boxes of ammunition, and a brand-new nickel-plated revolver.

The young man had experience with the small catboats of the Corinthian Yacht Club in Marblehead, Massachusetts, but having no responsibilities on this voyage other than to rest and build up his health, he left the sailing to others. The passenger naturally had gotten to know his hosts, Captain and Mrs. Nash, as well as something of the so-called colored (he was black) steward, who served him his meals and made his bed every day. This was Jonathan Spencer, native of Saint Vincent and, at age twenty-four, not much older than Monks but already married and with a child on the way. Monks had also gotten to know the man who had originally welcomed him onboard, the second-in-command, the mate, Thomas Bram. The mate, Monks later remembered, told him that he was a French Canadian from Nova Scotia with the ability to speak not only English and French but German, Russian, and Spanish, as well.

Monks also recalled Bram saying that, when hired by Nash five weeks previously, his savings had amounted to just fifty cents, but half of this had gone to the man who brought his kit to the wharf. Bram complained that Nash offered him just forty dollars a month, the advance of which Bram said he had already used to pay property taxes he owed in Brooklyn, New York. Bram also griped, Monks remembered, that Nash did not use enough sail, provided a poor table, and never allowed his men liquor. In response to the last hardship, one evening Monks dipped into his private reserve and shared a cup with both Bram and the third-in-command, the second mate. The second mate was August W. Blomberg, a large man, perhaps the largest man onboard. He was age thirty-two and originally from Finland; little else was known about him.

While getting along perfectly well in the afterhouse, Monks had no reason to venture eighty feet across the deck load to the forward house, and its denizens would never dare set foot in the afterhouse. According to the age-old customs of the sea, the afterhouse belonged to officers and other privileged persons, while the forward house belonged to the common sailor.

From the outside, the forward house resembled the afterhouse by being a small, four-sided, flat-roofed structure. Internally, though, the two houses were entirely different. While no interior description of the

Herbert Fuller's forward house seems to exist, inside it would have been a Spartan affair, consisting of such compartments as a galley for cooking; a cabin for the steward to sleep in; various lockers and chambers for provisions; a carpenter's shop; a bucket for urine and feces; and, up against the bow bulkheads, the forecastle. It was in such forecastles (renowned for their indescribable odors) where sailors took their grub, dried their gear in foul weather, told each other jokes and yarns, read and reread old newspapers and dime-store novels, smoked or chewed tobacco, and slept on hard and narrow bunks.

Before signing papers with the US shipping commissioner in Boston on July 1, the six men in the forecastle of the *Herbert Fuller* had been total strangers to each other. After having given notice at their respective boardinghouses, the men reported to Captain Nash on July 2, the day before departure, and they could plan on being gone many months, with Nash intending to sail from Argentina to Brazil for a return load of sugar. And upon return, the men could expect to be sacked. A competent steward such as Spencer might be invited to stay with the vessel (as indeed Spencer had been from a previous trip), but otherwise skippers like Nash preferred to engage their crew for the duration of the voyage only and not a day longer. This practice may have helped the bottom line for captains, but for sailors it meant a constant scramble for new work. To keep costs low, captains took on as few sailors as possible, two men per mast being the rule, and paid them poorly. In Nash's case, this amounted to twenty dollars a month, or about sixty-five cents a day.

A sailor's schedule was determined by which side of the forecastle he bunked. Sailors who bunked on the port side were assigned the port watch, while those who bunked on the opposite side were given the starboard watch. The two watches rotated duties on a four-hour basis, with the exception of the once-a-day "dog watch" of two hours. The watch that "stood" above deck worked the ship, while the watch that stood below deck relaxed or slept but was always liable to be summoned when all hands were needed topside. A pious captain might allow for a little rest on Sundays, but for sailors at sea, there was no such thing as a holiday.

The sailors' duties varied from the pleasant, such as standing lookout in fine weather, to the mundane, like the constant scrubbing with canvas and sand, to the disagreeable, such as "sweating up" heavy halyards or "weighing" tons of anchor. In addition, sailors faced the ever-present hazards of disease, accident, shipwreck, or fire, thus making their profession deadlier than that of a coal miner's.

Sailors also faced a man-made hazard, which was cruelty at the hands of their superiors, some of whom went in for violent hazing. Sadistic masters and mates could essentially do with their underlings as they pleased, knowing that sailors had no legal recourse while at sea and little more upon reaching shore, where an officer's word held greater weight than a lowly sailor's.

Not surprisingly, the life of a sailor held little appeal to most Americans, given the nature of the vocation and the fact that a better living, and one that promised some opportunity for promotion, could be had on land. At one time, master mariners had learned the trade by spending many years "before the mast" as common sailors in the forecastle. However, now captains like Nash increasingly were coming from shipowning families and had been handed their commands at a tender age. Most full (or chief) mates like Bram, with no family connections, could expect to remain at their present rank indefinitely. Poorly paid and overworked, it was the mate's lot to manage the ship, while the captain maintained an aloof presence. By comparison, second mates worked just as hard as mates yet were paid even less (Nash paid just thirty dollars a month). Worse, second mates could also be demoted to deckhand in an instant, with another man brought up in his stead. This meant that second mates were neither quite officer nor quite sailor and were often despised by both groups. And as if to remind second mates of their humble status, they did not eat with the men in the forecastle nor with the captain and mate in the afterhouse. Instead they swallowed their pride and made do with "second mate's seconds"—that is, leftovers from the captain's table.

Unable to attract its native sons, America's shipping industry had turned to others. By the 1890s nine out of ten men who shipped on the country's vessels came from abroad, and as it headed to the Argentine, nowhere was this more evident than onboard the *Herbert Fuller*. Only the captain, his wife, and the passenger were US born, and although the two mates (as required by US maritime law) and the steward were US citizens, they had been naturalized as such. As for the six sailors, all were foreign nationals. Francis "Frank" M. Loheac was French, Henry J. Slice was German, and Hendrik Perdok was Dutch. The other three, Charles "Charley" Brown, Falke Wassen, and Oscar Andersson, were

Swedish. The hard life of a sailor was a young man's game, and at age forty Brown was the "old man" of the group. Slice was age thirty, and the other four were in their early twenties.

Only some of the sailors spoke English, and not all shared a common language, but as the barkentine plowed the seas ahead, the six worked well together. They also worked well with their superiors, especially with Captain Nash, whom they all recalled afterward as a gentle man of quiet manners and easygoing ways. For his part, the captain informed his brother Henry, who had visited the *Herbert Fuller* while the vessel was still at Nantasket Roads, that he was "perfectly satisfied" with his new crew.

In a display of egalitarianism unusual in a captain, upon reaching the open seas, Nash took the time to ask his sailors where they thought the vessel was located, something that could not be determined with any precision because the night skies had been too hazy for a sextant shot of the heavens. By simply following the compass southwest, however, it would be hard for Nash to miss the continent of South America. And even if he did, there were enough provisions in the hold and enough fresh water in the iron tanks to last everyone onboard six months.

CHAPTER 2

By late Monday afternoon, July 13, the *Herbert Fuller* was about six or seven hundred miles from Boston, having just sliced through warm blue waters to emerge on the southern side of the Gulf Stream. For the past several days, life aboard the barkentine had gone on as before: perfectly normal, even mundane. The captain's wife had made sure things were kept spick-and-span in the afterhouse, the sailors had hung their laundry out to dry, someone had caught a dolphin and the steward had cooked it, and the passenger had kept to his schedule of constant rest. At six o'clock that evening, he was lounging on the deck load amidships and reading a book given to him by the captain when the call to supper sounded.

Heeding the call, Monks closed his book and made his way to the main cabin, where he was joined by Captain and Mrs. Nash and the mate, Bram. The small party took their respective places around the solid oak dining table and were served supper by Spencer. The Nashes were not ones for table talk, seldom speaking to one another (and never to first mates like Bram, who were expected to eat in silence), but for their guest's sake, the couple had been making an effort at conversation, and tonight they were more loquacious than usual. Mrs. Nash in particular seemed to enjoy the young man's company.

After supper, all went above, where the mate saw to the ship's business; the passenger resumed his reading amidships; and the married couple walked on the starboard side of the afterhouse roof, her hand gently resting on his arm. At one point, the passenger saw the mate,

Bram, come up to the couple, say something, and then turn away. Meanwhile, down in the main cabin, the second mate, Blomberg, was now permitted to partake of his second mate's seconds.

The book the captain had given Monks was *A Voyage to the Cape*, by William Clark Russell, famous author of harrowing sea stories, and the one now absorbing Monks told of the loss of the *Frank N. Thayer* of Boston in 1886. According to Russell's account:

> A large full-rigged ship was sailing quietly along. The starlight transmuted each ripple, rolling sluggishly away from her stem, into a line of silver wire. There was just enough draught to hold her sails steady. It was midnight—not a sound broke the stillness upon the vessel's decks, unless it were the low murmur of the voices of the first and second mates seated on the after-hatch, one exchanging a few words with the other before he went below. The master was in his cabin sound asleep. The starboard watch arrived on deck, took a lazy look around, and, as the custom of seamen is in fine, clear, warm weather, stowed themselves away under the bulwarks or under the lee of the long-boat for a nap, but ready for the first call from the quarter-deck.
>
> There were on board two Indian coolies who had been shipped at Manilla; one was in the port, the other in the starboard watch, and it was noticed by the port watch when they went below at midnight that the Indian belonging to their number remained on deck. The sailors had stowed themselves away, as I have said, and the mates were still conversing when the two coolies stepped aft, and both of them drawing close to the mates, one of them exclaimed that he felt sick. The speech was a signal; swift as thought the sharp knives of the Indians flashed and fell, again and yet again. The chief mate sank, mortally wounded; the second mate staggered to the cabin door, and calling out, "Captain Clarke! Captain Clarke!" fell dead.
>
> The master of the vessel being awakened by the second mate's cry of anguish, sprang from his bed and made for the steps of the after companion, his notion being that they were about to collide with a ship that had been sighted ahead at sundown, and that they had been steadily overhauling. Scarce had he gained the companion ladder when he was violently stabbed on the top of his head, and at the same moment a hand grasped his throat. He was in his night-dress and unarmed, and all that he could do was to strike fiercely at his assailant's eyes, hoping to blind him. The Indian however, unhurt, continued to stab at the captain, who descended the ladder step by step, striking out aimlessly and madly for his life. At the foot of the

steps he slipped in the blood that covered the treads, and fell headlong back into the cabin with a frightful wound in his left side. The Indian, supposing him to be dead, ran on deck, whereupon the captain crawled to where his revolver was, and again feebly staggered up the companion, and called to the man at the wheel to shut the door.

The fellow replied, "I can't sir."

"Why not?" cried the captain.

"There's somebody there," was the reply.

"Who is there?" demanded the captain.

"I don't know, sir," responded the fellow.

The master had his wife and child on board, and his first thoughts were for them. He could not imagine what had happened, but his idea was that the whole crew had mutinied, and that his life was to be sacrificed. He was faint and bleeding dreadfully, yet was crawling towards his wife's cabin when a man came rolling down the companion steps. He thought it was the Indian who had stabbed him; quickly turned and covered the figure with his revolver.

"What is the matter?" he cried. "Who are you? What is this mutiny about?"

The fellow proved to be one of the sailors, half paralyzed by terror. He crouched and knelt before the captain crying, "Oh, hide me, Captain! Hide me!" and that was all his agony of fright suffered him to say.

The master, believing himself to be fast bleeding to death, fell down on a mat in the corner of the cabin, yet ever with a trembling and languid hand holding his pistol levelled in the direction of the companion. His wife applied herself to staunch the blood and dress his wounds. Whilst this was doing the coolies smashed the skylight window, and one told the other in bastard Spanish to jump below. The captain fired at them, on which they rushed away, uttering many oaths and exhibiting great surprise and alarm. Very soon after they had vanished a dreadful cry was heard on deck, followed by a short scuffle, and it was known that the man at the wheel, a seaman named Malony, had been stabbed and flung overboard. This was followed by another cry, and then another. The cook, who was a Chinaman, and whose life the two coolies spared, afterwards declared these shrieks came from the carpenter and a seaman, both of whom the Indians had murdered.

Besides the slain men there were four whom the coolies had wounded. These fellows had run to the forecastle for protection, and here the ship's company barricaded themselves. They of course by this time knew that the murderers were but two slender, puny, Indian coolies, creatures whom an English Jack would be able to break the backs of by putting them against his knee. Yet these hardy Yankee mariners were so demoralized by terror that instead of arming themselves with a handspike or two and springing on deck and knocking out the brains of the brace of black villains they fortified their little forecastle, and lay in it trembling and panic-stricken. One of the sailors was left on deck.

"As I could not get forward," he says, "I ran up the mizzen rigging and got on to the crossjack yard. I then saw them kill Malony at the wheel. He offered no resistance, and I heard him beg hard for his life. I remained aloft, and saw them at two a.m. on Sunday murder the carpenter, and shortly afterwards they dragged a sailor from the carpenter's shop, murdered him near the mainmast, and threw him overboard. Having done this, they sharpened a couple of axes and fixed knives to long sticks with which they tried to stab the captain and his wife in the cabin. They wanted me to come down, but I knew they only asked me to do that in order to murder me. I had no knife with me, otherwise I should have cut off blocks and hurled them at the two coolies. I managed, however, to cast one block adrift, and secure it at the end of a gasket, so that I should have some weapon to use if the Indians approached me. At eight o'clock in the evening, it being then dark, I felt the rigging shake, and, looking below, I saw one of the coolies raising his arm to strike upwards at me. I hit at him with the block, but missed him, and he descended the rigging to the deck. This so terrified me that I climbed as high as the royal yard, and stayed there all night."

The coolies approaching the cabin skylight, one was shot in the breast by the captain. Both of them immediately rushed forward, threw a spare spar overboard, and one jumped into the sea, whilst the other dropped down into the 'tween decks. Seeing this, the sailor who was aloft came hand over fist down onto the deck, and shouted out to the captain to break out of the cabin. At the same moment the sailors ran out of the forecastle. Meanwhile the coolie in the 'tween decks was hard at work setting the ship on fire. Two seamen armed with revolvers jumped below to hunt him out, and they shot him in the shoulder; but by this time the smoke was pouring out densely from the hatchway, and the coolie, half hidden by it, gained the deck, and sprang overboard. Both wretches were seen in the water holding on to the spar; but shots were fired at them, and after a little they sank. The ship was on fire, and burning rapidly. There was no chance

> of saving her, so a boat was provisioned, the crew entered her, and after hanging about the ship during Monday night, in the hope that the flames would bring assistance, they put some blankets together for a sail and headed for St. Helena. The vessel was an American vessel, and the ship's company, who had been overawed and rendered helpless through terror by two miserable coolies, must have numbered at the beginning of the mutiny no less than twenty-three souls.

The sun having set, it became too dark to read, and so Monks closed his book and went below. Afterward he reckoned the time to be no later than eight o'clock, but planning to arise early as had become his custom at sea, he intended to turn in for the night. Inside the chart room he found Captain Nash reading, by the light of a lamp, a tome entitled *Three Gringos in Venezuela and Central America*, Mrs. Nash having retired for the evening. Passenger and captain chatted for about ten minutes before the passenger said goodnight and went into his adjoining stateroom.

The room had no light, but by keeping the door open to the rays of the chart room lamp, Monks could change into his yellow pajamas. When he finished changing, Monks shut his door and, he later testified, took care to lock it. Monks also testified that he was unsure if the door between his cabin and the adjoining stateroom where Mrs. Nash slept was locked but added that the door was shut as it had been since the start of the voyage and, on his side, he had placed one of his trunks up against it.

Monks now climbed onto his berth and, lying there in the darkness, would have listened to the sundry sounds of a sailing ship under way. Perhaps he heard the clank of the steering chain or the groan of the white pine cargo shifting in the swell. Or perhaps he listened to the splash of water against the hull or the creak of cordage and the flap of sails coming from somewhere on high. In any event, Monks fell into a deep slumber and just maybe dreamed of a "large full-rigged ship," "sailing quietly along," when the "master of the vessel" was "awakened by" a "cry of anguish."

"Sometime before daybreak I was aroused from my sleep," the young man later remembered. "I did not then know what time it was, but I have since come to believe it was about two o'clock. I was awakened by a scream, a shrill scream, and I sat up in bed. Then I heard nothing for a few moments, and after that I heard a horrible noise coming apparently from the chart room. It sounded as though somebody was strangling. I called out 'Captain Nash! Captain Nash!' but got no answer."

Then, Monks recalled, he reached down and opened the drawer under his bunk; took out a box of cartridges; and, from underneath his pillow, grasped his revolver. Arising from his mattress, he loaded his gun and put on a pair of slippers (yellow to match his pajamas).

"I listened awhile and still heard the screaming," Monks recollected, "and then I unlocked the door and stepped into the chart room."

The lamp there had gone out, but he could see somewhat from the light of the swinging lantern, its wick turned low, coming through the passageway to the main cabin. The captain's mattress and cot, he could tell, had been overturned, and the captain, dressed in pajamas, lay on the carpet.

"I thought he had tipped over from his bed. I went up to him, looked at his head, and put my hand first on his head and then on his shoulder. He did not move."

Seeking help from Mrs. Nash, Monks dashed to the main cabin and then the few feet to her room. Her door was unlocked.

"It was very dark," Monks recalled. "I found her bed and could see dark splashes on her sheets. As soon as I saw those, I realized they were blood splashes and that the scream I had heard meant something. I retraced my steps in order to get out of the cabin as soon as possible and went out to the after companionway, with the intention of going on deck."

At the top of the companionway was the door to the afterdeck. Six hours earlier, when Monks had gone to bed, this door had definitely been open, but now he saw that it was shut. Fearing that there might be someone on the other side "who would strike me," he dared not find out. Although later claiming to have never been scared, the young man nevertheless spun around and sought his escape via the forward companionway. Here the door at the top of the stairs was open and no enemies were evident. He ventured partway up the stairs but stopped midway, so that his lower body remained below the deck load of lumber while his upper body was above. Monks later reckoned about ten minutes had passed since he had heard the first scream.

"I looked out to the deck and saw Mr. Bram walking up and down," Monks remembered. "It was a warm night, cloudy, and I think no moon." Bram, standing just ten feet away, picked up a piece of board and threw it at Monks. The board missed and rattled down the companionway.

Monks said, "Don't throw that board at me. I'm alright," and then added, "For God's sake, come below. The captain has been murdered."

"No, no, no, no," replied Bram.

"Come below," Monks repeated, "and see for yourself."

Monks stepped all the way up and onto the deck load and then, following the mate, back down. At the foot of the forward companionway and on the right was Bram's cabin, and Monks remembered that they stopped there and that he asked Bram if he had a revolver. Bram said yes, he had a revolver and some ammunition. Monks told Bram to go in and get both, which Bram did. Monks also recalled that Bram had on the same attire he had worn since leaving Long Wharf, which was a white straw hat with a hole in the crown, a black coat and a black shirt with a white stripe, trousers, and slippers made of carpet.

Monks, however, was still in his pajamas, and he told Bram that he wanted to go to his room and change. To light their way through the interior of the afterhouse, Bram took down the swinging lantern from the partition above the dining table and turned the wick up high. With Monks following, he went into the chart room and then to the passenger's cabin. Monks entered and placed the lantern on the floor but near the door so that Bram, standing just outside in the chart room, could have some light, too.

Monks began changing into a pair of cotton duck trousers and a flannel shirt when Bram began to move away from sight. Monks recalled saying, "Come back and stay here," which Bram did.

Now properly attired, Monks left the lantern, still at full blaze, where it was on the floor. Bram retraced their steps through the chart room and into the main cabin and then to the foot of the forward companionway. According to Monks, he said not a word to Bram during their exit, including nothing about having looked into Mrs. Nash's room and what he had seen there.

The two ran up the steps and onto the deck load, where they hunkered down at the temporary rail near the mizzenmast rigging amidships. Monks asked what time it was, and Bram answered that he didn't know, saying that someone had set the afterhouse clock back. From their vantage point amidships, Monks could discern in the darkness that two men were also topside, one at the wheel behind the afterhouse and another occasionally visible walking back and forth near the forward house head. Monks asked Bram where "Blum"—the nickname given to the second mate, August Blomberg—was, and, according to Monks, Bram answered that he was "forward with the crew and that all had mutinied."

Then, according to Monks, Bram "began to cry and put his arms around my knees and asked me to protect him, that he had been hard on the crew and they would kill him. He then said he was sick and that he had got some whiskey from the second mate at twelve o'clock and that the second mate told him he had got it from me."

According to Monks, Bram said he had thrown the cup overboard but thought the drink had been drugged. Bram then vomited on deck, and Monks advised him to get up and walk around.

"He staggered around the deck and then sat down again," Monks later testified. "He had walked perfectly natural when he had been downstairs. On deck he staggered a good deal and leaned on me."

According to Monks, Bram recuperated after Monks told him "to brace up," and the two sat down again by the railing, Monks instructing Bram to cover the man at the wheel with his revolver, while he would cover the man ahead. Monks recalled saying that the steward should be woken in the galley, but Bram warned that, if they did, then the men would come out of the forecastle and attack them.

"Bram talked a good deal about protection," Monks recalled, and the two of them remained where they were amidships, both pointing their guns in opposite directions, with Monks expecting the mutineers to rush aft at any minute.

The night, Monks remembered, "was cloudy but not absolutely thick," and he could see the occasional star flickering in the sky above. When the first signs of daylight appeared around four o'clock and nothing had happened, the passenger and mate approached the outside galley door at the rear of the forward house and rapped loudly. Spencer, dressed only in trousers, appeared and gave the mate a mock salute. For the second time that morning, Monks delivered news that their captain had been murdered.

"Oh, I guess not," Spencer replied.

"Look for yourself," said Monks.

The three went aft, where Spencer, Monks remembered, stood on the afterhouse roof and peered through the skylight. Seeing the captain's prone and lifeless body below, Spencer, a lithe and athletic young man, rushed down the companionway and then rushed up a few minutes later with the news that the second mate lay dead in his bunk.

"I thought you said Blum was forward," Monks said to Bram.

"Well, he was forward," Bram responded.

Bram turned and asked Spencer if he had a revolver. Spencer answered no, and Bram gave him his and then told Monks, "Give me yours."

"I will not," Monks replied.

Ensuring that Bram's revolver worked, Spencer aimed over the side and pulled the trigger. The gun went off, and Bram jumped. Spencer pulled the trigger again, but this time there was just a click. The steward opened the cylinder and inspected the shells. He saw that all the unused ones were nicked, indicating they had been struck by the hammer at some previous time but failed to fire.

The trio happened upon the vomit that Bram spat up earlier. Monks and Spencer thought a sample should be preserved for analysis, but before this could happen, according to Monks, Bram slid into the bile and wiped it up with his carpet slippers. A more momentous discovery came at the starboard side of the ship, near the rail opposite the main mast, when Bram pointed down.

"There is the ax that did it!" he cried out.

The other two noticed nothing at first but, their gaze following the direction of Bram's finger about ten feet further, saw the storeroom ax, its handle bearing the unmistakable print of a bloody hand, shoved in under a lashing plank.

"Either Mr. Bram or the steward picked it up. I don't remember which one of them," Monks said later. "And then Bram had the ax in his hands, and he began to grin and cry over it—sort of a hysterical grin. He said, 'What shall we do with it? Shall we throw it overboard?' And I said 'Yes, because if we don't, the crew will use it against us.'"

Spencer protested, "No, you should not do that," but Bram gave out a yell and tossed the murder weapon into the sea.

The three promptly marched aft and to the back of the afterhouse, where on the stern deck the sailor Frank Loheac had the wheel. With the barrels of two revolvers pointed directly at his head, Loheac claimed ignorance of having witnessed anything out of the ordinary. The trio left the startled Frenchman to his steering but not before informing him that their captain had been murdered.

Reversing course, Monks, Spencer, and Bram trooped up to the forward house. In front of the house, Monks recalled, they found two sailors, Charley Brown, the Swede, who spoke limited English, and a stout fellow with a red face whom everyone called Bill, but whose real name (Hendrik Perdok, the Dutchman) Monks did not know, who spoke no English. Spencer told Brown to go below and bring whomever was down there up, and soon all the sailors except for Loheac, still aft at the wheel, were gathered on the fore deck.

The interrogation began.

"When did you see the second mate last?" they were asked.

Some said at eight o'clock the previous evening, some said twelve midnight. After being told what happened, the sailors looked shocked and, like Loheac, insisted they knew nothing. The mystery unsolved, everyone moved aft and, except for Monks, took turns inspecting the interior of the afterhouse. "I got as far as the second mate's door and turned around and came back," Monks admitted. "I saw the second mate in there, all cut up."

By this time the bodies of Captain and Mrs. Nash had also been found, their unspeakable wounds confirming death by ax, too.

After viewing the ghastly results of this carnival of murder, the nine survivors clustered on top of the deck load and asked, "Who among us could have done this fiendish deed?" Given the horrific, unimaginable events that had just transpired, all onboard were in a state of extreme excitement. Spencer began naming possible suspects and settled, for some reason, on the German sailor Henry Slice, before dropping him as a plausible culprit.

Then Bram, according to Monks, began crying about his poor old mother and how the captain was a Freemason and how he also was a Freemason. He then explained his theory of how the murders took place.

"He said the way this thing had happened, that the second mate had gone to make an assault on Mrs. Nash and that the captain woke up and got the ax and had gone in and struck the second mate," Monks said later. "And then the second mate had got the ax from the captain and killed the captain and then killed Mrs. Nash, and then the second mate had staggered on deck and left the ax and gone back to his bunk."

Monks recalled Bram as also saying, "We mustn't blame the living for the dead. The dead cannot speak for themselves. We will take the bodies up and throw them overboard and wash up the blood."

Spencer again thought that no evidence should be discarded and said, "No, no, we will leave them just where they are."

Monks agreed. "Of course," he said and then added, "We have got to make the nearest port possible."

Monks asked Bram where that port might be, and Bram suggested Cayenne in French Guiana.

Following a brief discussion, all agreed to sail there, but what should they do with the bodies? Stored upside down on top of the forward house were two utility boats, a smaller one called the jolly boat and a larger one called the long boat. Slice suggested the bodies be put in the smaller one.

Again, Spencer argued against disturbing anything, but the rest thought it a good idea, and so the men went about the morbid task of hauling the butchered and bleeding corpses up on deck, work made marginally more palatable by covering the hacked faces of the victims with towels. The captain, his wife, and the second mate were heavy folk, and each required all six sailors to handle, with Bram supervising. In the interim, the passenger volunteered to man the wheel. After about fifteen minutes, though, Monks had allowed the ship to go into the wind, and Slice had to dash to the helm and rescue the situation.

At a time of day normally reserved for breakfast, the crew sewed the victims up in sheets and quilts taken from the afterhouse and began to prepare the makeshift sarcophagus for its future occupants. The living released the jolly boat from the forward house roof, turned it upright on its keel, and lashed it to the surface of the deck load between the main and fore masts. To protect the cadavers from the elements, they prepared layers of tarred canvas, which acted as a liner inside the boat and as a cover on top. With the sailors engaged in this labor, Monks went below for his cigars and when he returned asked Bram to take one and pass the rest around. Bram then requested that Monks write an account of the tragedy for the record. On five pieces of stationery taken from a New York hotel, the Harvard man grasped a lead pencil and wrote out with imperfect spelling:

Tuesday, July 14, 1896

Monday night everything on board the barkentine Herbert Fuller was perfectly quiet and peaceful. The crew had no fault to find with anything on board. The second mate had the watch from 8 to 12. I went to bed about 8 o'clock. The steward says the captain had been drinking, but I did not notice it. I am naturally a very heavy sleeper, so the murders which were committed might have happened before I woke up.

My first recollections are these: I heard a scream, followed by a gurlling noise, as if someone was choking. I reached down and got a box of shells, took my revolver and filled the pistol, which I kept under my pillow, as fast as possible. Then I called, "Captain Nash." As I got no answer I unlocked my cabin door and stepped out into the after cabin.

The captain slepted on a cot placed against the starboard wall. The captain was lying on the floor with the couch tipped upon end. I went up to him and shook him. I found he was covered with blood. I ran into Mrs. Nash's room to call her.

I could see that sheets of her bunk were covered with blood. I then ran forward to the forward companionway and looked on the deck. I saw the mate, Mr. Bram, on deck. I called to him and held my revolver pointed toward him.

When he saw me, he picked up a board to throw at me, but I called out: "It's me—Mr. Bram; come below for God's sake."

He came below, and we took the lantern in the forward cabin and went into the after cabin. I slipped on a pair of trousers and a shirt; he grabbed his revolver, and we ran on deck. We did not know who were our friends or foes. We crouched down on the deck to windard just abreast of the mizzenmast.

Mr. Bram covered the man at the wheel, and I kept my revolver pointed forwards. It was very dark. In this way we sat waiting for daylight.

We then went forward and banged on the galley door for the steward, J. Spencer. He came on deck, and we told him what had happened. He went aft and went into the cabin, while Bram and myself kept on deck with our revolvers.

He came running out of the cabin in a few minutes and said [unclear] second mate, Mr. Blum, was lying dead in his berth. We then went aft in a body and questioned the man at the wheel. He said he didn't know anything had happened, and had heard no unusual noises.

> We then went forward and woke up the crew. They all appeared greatly astonished and all protested they knew nothing.
>
> We all then went aft in a body and went into the cabin. The second mate was lying dead in his bunk. Mrs. Nash was lying in her bunk with her clothes pulled up. Captain Nash was lying on the floor dead. We went on deck and at once decided to steer for French Cayane, that being the nearest port.
>
> My theory of the tragedy is this:
>
> The second mate, Mr. Blum, had been drinking, and went below and tried to rape Mrs. Nash. Captain Nash woke up and went and got an ax (the one we threw overboard) and attempted to kill Blum and his wife. Blum must off gotten the axe and hit the captain and then staggered on deck and then back to his bunk.

After writing the above, Monks realized he had missed a detail and scribbled in a margin,

> We found a bloody ax on the deck which we threw overboard, as we feared the crew would use it against us

Having completed his account, he signed it,

> Lester Hawthorne Monks

Then, however, the author thought to add a postscript and wrote,

> The second mate offered Mr. Bram a drink at about 12 o'clock. This whiskey made Mr. Bram very sick while on deck with me, and he acted as if he had been drugged.

The author's account finally complete, he read it aloud and when finished signed it for a second time and was followed by the rest of the survivors:

> Lester Hawthorne Monks
> Thomas H. Bram, Mate
> Jonathan Spencer
> Charles Brown
> Frank Loheac
> Falke Wassen

There being no more room on that side of the paper, the remaining men signed their names in a single line on the reverse side:

Henry J. Slice Oscar Andersson Hendrik Perdok

The jolly boat having been made ready, the somber moment had come to intern the mortal remains of the recently departed. Although professing not to be a religious man, Monks declared that a Christian burial service was in order and produced a copy of the Episcopal prayer book. Bram ordered the organ be brought up so he could play a hymn for the occasion, but the sailors, perhaps having hauled enough heavy items out of the afterhouse for one day, started but then abandoned the effort. The ensuing ceremony, therefore, consisted just of Monks reading from the Order of the Dead. "I am the resurrection and the life, Saithe the Lord," Monks began, before quitting a few lines later.

That done with, the sailors lifted the three bodies into the jolly boat and placed the second mate to port, the captain amidships, and the captain's wife to starboard, such that she could be next to her husband.

CHAPTER 3

No sooner had the tarred canvas been nailed down over the jolly boat than Bram assumed command of the *Herbert Fuller*. He immediately appointed Brown mate and Loheac second mate and then asked all the men to shake his hand. Navigation became the next order of business. Bram and Loheac went into the afterhouse and rummaged through the charts kept by the late Captain Nash before emerging topside with an old one of the Atlantic. The numbers and lines had faded over the years, but after examining the map, Bram declared their position to be about 1,500 miles from Cayenne, an eight-day voyage should they catch the northwest trade winds.

Huddled around the chart, however, the men asked: Why not just sail to Bermuda, less than five hundred miles away? Bram explained that, despite recent events, they still had an obligation to deliver the white pine to Rosario and that Cayenne was on the way. Never mind the white pine, the others protested, demanding that they just get ashore, anywhere, as soon as possible. Bram had no objections but did point out that, from their present location, it would take a month to sail to Bermuda because they would be beating against prevailing headwinds the entire way.

He instead suggested Halifax, Nova Scotia, an easier sail with favorable winds of about 750 miles. With Monks being the most enthusiastic, all readily agreed, and so within thirty minutes the *Herbert Fuller* had been brought about, kept to the port tack while close-hauled to the wind, and set on a course to eastern Canada.

Although every man onboard had just endorsed Monks's theory of the murders, none of them, including Monks, believed a word of it, and all had no doubt that the maniac responsible still lurked among them. The mutual suspicion that had existed onboard that morning continued all afternoon, with the men eyeing each other nervously and exchanging various ideas about how the butchery took place. Additionally, they scoured all corners of the vessel for clues that might have some bearing on the crime but by nightfall had come no closer to solving the mystery. Fearing a repeat of last night's performance, the men sawed the handles off all remaining axes on board; did likewise to the boat-hook handles; and nailed the carpenter's shop, with all of its sharp tools, shut.

Despite these precautions and trusting no one but themselves, Bram, Monks, and Spencer frisked the six sailors and allowed them no weapons other than their sheath knives. Once searched, the sailors were ordered to bunk out in the open between the fore and main masts, while Bram, Spencer, and Monks, with their two revolvers, would keep station atop the afterhouse. Dawn appeared after a warm July night with no further mayhem having taken place, though surely no one slept well.

At one point later that day, the Dutch-speaking Perdok (presumably with someone translating) came up to Bram and said, "You should watch Charley Brown."

"What is wrong?"

"Well, Charley is very peculiar."

Perdok said that, on the night of the murders, Brown had taken his mattress out of the forward house and put it beneath the long boat on the roof, having never done that before, and seemed to have been busy doing something under there. Perdok also said, "And last night, when myself and Oscar Andersson were sleeping, he came over to us a good many times and peeped into our faces and tell us to go to sleep."

The other sailors then informed Bram that all day Brown had avoided them and instead walked around scratching his head and talking to himself, his eyes wild and bloodshot. Just now, the sailors continued, Brown came up to them and said he had seen "those people who were killed," and when he started to go forward, "they" would go with him, and when he came back, "they" would be with him.

More unsettling news arrived when the new second mate, Loheac, advised Bram to lock the forepeak hatch leading down to the barrel of kerosene.

"Why?" Bram asked.

"Take my advice and lock it. Charley Brown was speaking of how easy it would be to set the vessel afire."

The evidence piled up and the decision was made to arrest Brown. The sequence of events was captured in Bram's logbook entry for sea day July 15 (noon Tuesday, July 14, to noon Wednesday, July 15, on land).

> Wednesday, day of 15 July, 1896.
>
> On this day at 5.30 P.M. the steward of said H. Fuller came to me and told me that the sailors all came and made an open statement to him in reference to one of the sailor's whose name is Charles Brown's conduct of guilt in regard to the murder which took place on board said vessil. I at once got each men's statement; then upon the strength of these statements we came to the conclusion to put him in irons at daybreak. At 7 p m all hands was musterd aft and thoroughly searcht. No other wepon was given them but their knives. Each man was then placed a certin distance apart from each untop of the after house. Myself, the steward and passenger was stationed amidships well armed, and kept a good lookout untile daybreak. A 5 a m Charles Brown was mancled and put in irons. His actions all night was very suspicious and got himself all ready, as it were, to jump over the side, but he was well guarded by all hands on board. At 1.30 a. m. he made a desperate rush for the forward part of the ship, but was instantly stop by the steward upon a pointed revolver towards him. Moderate weather winds & seas.

Logbook entries did not require a signature, but Bram thought this particular one did, and so he read it aloud and asked each man to follow him in signing it. Monks, however, objected to the word *desperate* because in his opinion Brown's rush forward had been more deliberate than desperate, so Bram changed the word to *effort* such that the last line now read,

> At 1.30 a. m. he made an effort rush for the forward part of the ship . . .

That detail taken care of, no one could think of another reason not to endorse the logbook entry, and so all, except for Perdok, who had the wheel, and of course Brown, who was in irons, signed below what Bram had written.

Brown's arrest had come in the wee hours of the morning after a night of bizarre behavior on his part. At one point Brown appeared ready to jump overboard, hundreds of miles from shore, by taking off his hat, shirt, and shoes and also by looking over the railing on either side of the ship. At another point, and after being warned like all the sailors to remain on the afterhouse roof, Brown had rushed toward the bow (the action that Monks had thought deliberate), only to be confronted by Spencer and his revolver. Stymied in whatever it was he intended to do, Brown finally settled down on the afterhouse roof next to the skylight and slept with an oilskin coat over his head.

At the first sign of light, Spencer had solemnly declared, "Mr. Bram, it is getting daybreak now, and we will put that man in irons."

The rest of the crew gathered before sneaking up on Brown as he lay sleeping. Cursing, Spencer grabbed him, while Bram ordered Loheac to go below and fetch a pair of irons. After first roping Brown to the mizzenmast, the men transferred him to a well in the deck load where the lumber had been parted to access the mainsheet lines, and it was in that hole where Brown would languish for the rest of the barkentine's journey. Although the murderer had now been seized and secured, Spencer believed Brown could not have acted alone. Relinquishing his cooking duties so that he might keep watch on the sailors, Spencer asked Monks if he could have his new nickel-plated revolver, and Monks complied. The five sailors were also racked by fear, and none wanted to stand duty alone.

Since leaving Boston, the hazy skies had prevented sextant shots from being taken at night, making it impossible to determine the barkentine's exact position. Now, however, the heavens had cleared, and on Thursday, July 16, Bram recorded the vessel as being N 42°06' and W 55°30', or about 440 miles from Halifax. After a day of moderate waves and strong winds, more sextant readings were taken on Friday, and now the distance to the city had shrunk to two hundred miles, less than a day away.

The warm July weather had been a boon to the sailors when forced to sleep out on deck, but it had done nothing to preserve the contents of the jolly boat. An unpleasant odor began drifting over the *Herbert Fuller*. On Saturday morning, July 18, when the stench had become unbearable, the men unleashed the jolly boat from the deck load so that it could be towed a good distance astern. The sailors affixed a four-inch line to the jolly boat and, with Monks reading aloud from the New Testament, carefully lowered it over the leeward side.

As soon as the jolly boat began floating in the sea, however, the line securing it to the *Herbert Fuller* developed a kink. Knowing that the kink might cause the line to break, Bram called all hands to haul the line in for untangling. In order to free the helmsmen to help with this work, Bram brought the barkentine close to the wind and put the wheel in beckets (tying and anchoring two lines to the wheel's spokes to keep it stationary), which kept the barkentine on the same course. After fifteen minutes, when the jolly boat line had been untangled, the helmsmen returned to his post, unleashed the wheel, and the barkentine no longer steered of its own accord.

That evening the wind died down to nothing, and the heat below deck became so oppressive the men sought relief topside. But there they would get no rest. In the darkness the sailors swore they could hear horrible groans and screams coming from the jolly boat drifting astern. Then around midnight Spencer became alarmed by the cracking of a whip from somewhere on the starboard side. All listened intently and heard the cracking themselves and then heard it no more.

For the tormented souls of the *Herbert Fuller*, daylight could not come soon enough, and when it did, they were greeted by a welcome sight: land. Working over the faded map of the Atlantic with his parallel ruler and divider, Bram identified this as Sable Island, barren home to lighthouse keepers and wild horses, a hundred miles east of Halifax. The barkentine, becalmed in a glassy sea, had made little progress over the past twenty-four hours. But then a fresh breeze arose at around eight o'clock the next morning, Sunday, July 19, and Bram had the anchors readied for Halifax Harbor.

The *Herbert Fuller*'s logbook, kept current since the vessel's launch in Harrington six years earlier, abruptly stops with mention of Sable Island and fails to record the sighting of a steamer shortly before noon. The steamer, a Canadian tramp flying the British ensign and set on a course for Boston, had appeared to port about six miles away. Neither Bram nor Spencer thought to bother the steamer now that they had a good wind for Halifax, but Monks insisted they signal it and tell those onboard of the murders. Doing as Monks requested, Bram attempted to get the steamer's attention by first hanging the Stars and Stripes upside down and then by having the sailors man the hand-cranked fog horn.

The efforts succeeded in stopping the steamer, but with its engines idled, it kept a wary distance.

"Haven't you any signals to send up indicating mutiny?" the impatient Monks asked Bram.

Below, in his stateroom, Bram had a brand-new book of international codes, and he brought it up on deck. He could not find a code for *mutiny* but did find one for *want assistance* and ordered the appropriate flags run up the mizzen signal halyards. The Canadian tramp took in the strange sights and sounds emanating from the Yankee barkentine for about twenty minutes and then steamed away.

Standing on top of the afterhouse roof with Captain Nash's spyglass pressed to his eye, Bram watched the ship disappear over the horizon and had no notion that Spencer stood right behind him with the passenger's revolver. Grabbing Bram by the throat, Spencer threw him down backward. As the rest of the men crowded around, Bram asked, "What is this for?"

"For these people that are killed," answered Spencer as he pointed the end of the revolver at the tip of Bram's nose.

Bram next found himself in irons and, with rope from the same spool used on Brown, lashed to the main mast. At twelve noon the sea day jumped to July 20, and an hour later Spencer brought Bram his dinner.

Said Bram, "Steward, I am an entirely innocent man. I know nothing about this crime."

"Mr. Bram, I don't believe you killed those people, but you ought to know something about it. Being on deck, you should have heard something."

The dead captain's rifle, an old and rusty affair, had already been found, but Spencer knew the captain also kept a well-maintained revolver onboard, and this was still missing. Convinced Bram had stolen it, Spencer broke into Bram's trunk but found nothing more incriminating than clothing and letters of recommendation from former employers.

The mystery was solved, however, when the revolver was discovered by either Loheac or Wassen (accounts vary) later that day in the passenger's cabin. The gun, a large .44-caliber weapon, was fully loaded and had been stashed between the two thin mattresses of the bunk Monk had slept on for a fortnight.

After Bram was given his supper that evening, Monks, always ready with a cigar, offered him a smoke. After darkness fell, they moved the shackled man to the stern, brought his mattress up from the afterhouse, and tied him to the bitts normally used to keep the spanker sheets fast.

The winds, which until then had been favorable for Halifax, died down when the *Herbert Fuller* got closer to shore, and by daylight on Monday, July 20, the city lay nowhere in sight. Again, the men moved Bram, this time to the forward house galley, where, his wrists still cuffed by irons, he took his parallel ruler and divider to the old chart of the Atlantic, setting a course for his jailors of northwest by west, half-west, forty-five miles to Halifax.

Convinced that Bram was lying, Spencer yelled out for directions a short while later when the barkentine came upon some fishing boats from New England. Yelling back, the skipper of the closest boat confirmed, "Northwest by west, half-west, forty-five miles to Halifax."

Rain fell throughout the day, and Spencer allowed Bram to remain in his galley but at the price of a little humiliation.

"Mate, the captain knew you were a colored man," the steward taunted, adding that he had even overhead the captain's wife talking about it.

Then the steward launched into a topic he evidently had been thinking about at great length. "Mr. Bram, if you had taken this vessel into port you would get nothing for it," Spencer argued, "but by we taking her in, they ought to give us at least five hundred dollars apiece for our trouble."

Bram, however, disagreed. "I have known cases where the mate has been paid by the insurance company for bringing vessels into port, but they have been dismasted, and part of the crew have fallen overboard—the captain and some of the crew—and the mate brought the vessel in. I know of one instance, the city of Philadelphia, a three-masted schooner, where the insurance company had paid him fifteen hundred dollars for bringing the vessel in."

Bram explained, however, that those had been "different circumstances" than the one the *Herbert Fuller* now found itself in and that "under these circumstances you would get nothing."

"I'm not looking for anything," Spencer snapped, before suggesting that Captain Nash's people at least ought to pay them something for bringing the bodies to port. Indeed, Spencer became quite heated on the subject of salvage rights, and for the next several hours, Bram could hear him and the sailors vowing that, if they had to, they would take their case to court.

That night a shirtless Bram again spent the dark hours in the stern lashed to the bitts, a rain soaking him to the bone. Daybreak found the *Herbert Fuller* lost in a fog, but then at around six o'clock, from out of the mists a rowboat appeared. The boat carried two pilots from Halifax Harbor, just six miles away, and as the pilots neared the barkentine, Spencer leaned over the rail and cautioned, "Be careful of that boat astern, as it contains corpses."

One of the pilots asked to speak with the captain. Spencer replied, "There has been murder aboard."

CHAPTER 4

The Halifax authorities took charge of the *Herbert Fuller* and stationed it in the anchorage opposite the insane asylum. By noontime the government cutter *Argus* had landed the barkentine's nine survivors onto Queens Wharf. From there they were escorted the few blocks to the majestic Halifax City Hall while being trailed by a large and excited crowd that included a reporter who managed to get the essential details from one of the nine.

This was a well-dressed young fellow named Lester Monks, who informed the reporter that he was a Harvard student from Boston and a passenger onboard and that the captain, his wife, and the second mate had been murdered with an ax. After the murders, Monks explained, he had personally taken command of the vessel, had ordered the arrest of the first mate on suspicion of murder, and had then navigated the ship to Halifax. While the crowd clustered about the "*Fuller* men," as they would soon be called, an equally large and excited throng gathered on Market Wharf to watch as the undertaker John Snow and his assistants peeled the canvas off the jolly boat and released a stench so powerful that it drove the nearest onlookers away. Inside the jolly boat and above a pool of green slime lay three silent forms encased in white shrouds.

The cadavers were transported to Snow's establishment on Argyle Street, where soon men, women, and children by the hundreds would surge through the door to get a good look. The sight, however, proved too ghastly for some, and they had to be helped outside. It was all terrible and terribly exciting. Indeed, the city had not been so transfixed by a crime since 1844, when six mariners from the *Saladin*, laden with seventy tons of copper, thirteen bars of silver, and nine thousand dollars in specie, were brought to Halifax to account for the mysterious disappearance of the captain, mate, second mate, three sailors, and two passengers.

The city's police chief, a man named John O'Sullivan, who spoke with the brogue of his native Ireland, made Monks as comfortable as possible. City hall doubled as police headquarters, and O'Sullivan turned his private office into an apartment for the young man's use and then asked what else he might do. Monks requested a telegram be sent to Boston, and soon the message SHIP AT HALIFAX COME AT ONCE would prompt the young man's father, Franklin Monks, and his uncle, Dr. George H. Monks, to purchase tickets for the next train to Nova Scotia. Joining them on the train departing that evening was Captain Wilber S. Nash of the bark *Elmita*, brother of one of the victims, and John Swann of Swann & Son of New York, agent and part owner of the *Herbert Fuller*.

Later during his almost-surreal first day ashore, Tuesday, July 22, the Harvard student was "put on the rack" by Chief O'Sullivan and Detective Nicholas Power, as well as by US Consul General Darius H. Ingraham, the American envoy in Halifax.

Lester Monks told his inquisitors of being woken by screams sometime around two o'clock on the morning of Tuesday, July 14; of retrieving and loading his revolver; of venturing from his room and finding Captain Nash on the floor; of trying to alert Mrs. Nash; of calling out to Bram from the companionway; and of all the other things he had done and seen until the seizure of the sailor Charley Brown on suspicion of murder, Wednesday, July 15.

Monks explained that, after being seized, Brown insisted he knew nothing of the crime, but then on the morning of Saturday, July 19, after forty-eight hours of captivity and constantly being berated by Spencer, Brown finally broke down. He confessed to seeing the mate, Thomas Bram, kill Captain Nash. Monks shared this startling news with Spencer, and the two decided that Bram could no longer have control of the *Herbert Fuller* and must be placed in irons. Monks then related the rest of his story, a story in which he played the leading role, culminating with the vessel's arrival in Halifax that very morning. Thanking Monks for his full cooperation, O'Sullivan, Power, and Ingraham left so the young man could get some rest. Exhausted and also secure in the knowledge that a policeman guarded his door, the hero began to catch up on his sleep.

The next day the policeman allowed in a visitor, and Monks had the chance to tell his version all over again, only this time it ran as front-page news.

"Young Monks is an exceedingly good looking and frank appearing young fellow, and a typical Harvard man in tone and action," Thomas F. Anderson, Canadian correspondent for Boston's two largest newspapers, the *Globe* and the *Herald*, began. "He was attired in a neat suit of light pattern, wore low cut shoes, and puffed away on a cigarette as he sat on a lounge as calmly as if he were discussing the latest yacht race off Marblehead."

When asked how he felt after his first night's sleep in over a week, Monks said he felt like a new man. "I never really knew the true value of sleep until last night," he told the correspondent. "To go eight days and nights is hard enough, but when it is accompanied, as in my case, by the knowledge that in wakefulness alone lies the hope of life, the mental and physical condition of the one who suffers is scarcely to be described."

According to the correspondent, the young fellow's "personal opinion is that mate Bram first killed the second mate, next the captain and finally the captain's wife, but like everybody else he is still mystified as to the real part played in the tragedy by the helmsman Brown. That an ordinary human being such as Brown with all the superstition that goes with the makeup of the average jack tar, could witness the commission of such an awful murder and for two days give no sign, almost passes belief."

Monks attempted to explain Brown's reluctance, telling the correspondent, "It may be, however, that the man was simply a coward and that his fears of possible consequences to himself were sufficient to restrain him."

While saying that he couldn't swear an oath as to who killed the three victims, Monks also said, "I firmly believe it was Bram," and he believed that Bram had done so while intoxicated by whiskey.

The correspondent then asked Monks if Bram's larger motives were not piratical, specifically to steal the valuable cargo of white pine boards. By killing the captain and second mate, according to one scenario that had gained credence in the press, Bram would have remained the only person onboard capable of navigating the ship (with the possible exception of Mrs. Nash, so perhaps that's why she, too, had to die). Bram could then have sailed the barkentine anywhere he so pleased, having violently dispatched with the passenger before bringing the crew into his plan.

According to this same scenario, the pirates' most likely destination would have been Cuba, where, at some secluded cove on the south side of the island, they could have sold the white pine to the Cuban insurrectionists (assuming the insurrectionists had a need for white pine), before vanishing with their ill-gotten gains forever.

Monks agreed, "It would have been easy to convince the seamen, who were a mixed and rather ignorant lot, that such a scheme could be worked, but Bram must have known that the thing was practically impossible."

"Resuming his rather disjointed narrative of the week of horror," Anderson wrote, "young Monks dwelt with feeling upon the dread uncertainty as to the outcome of the affair that rested upon his mind night and day.

"'There I was,' said he, 'in the midst of a miscellaneous crew of seamen, representing half a dozen different nationalities, one of them to my almost certain knowledge a red-handed murderer of the most fiendish character imaginable, another whom I half suspected of being at least an accomplice and only one of the lot whom I felt I could really trust, that of the colored steward.'"

In the interview, Monks also confided, "I was not one whit relieved, I can assure you, when the full conviction that Bram was probably the author of the diabolical butchery dawned upon me. Later followed the discovery that he was playing fast and loose with us in sailing the vessel. I do not pretend to know a great deal about navigation, but it did not take me long to discover what he was up to, and with that knowledge to take things wholly into my own hands and head the bark for the nearest port."

Amazed, here the correspondent remarked, "Your experience reads like Clark Russell's romances of the sea."

"Well now that brings up [a] strange coincidence," Monks replied. "The very evening before the murder, I had been reading one of Clark Russell's stories, in which a lot of Malays rise up [to] murder the captain of the vessel. I little dreamed that within a few short hours I myself would be an actor in an almost similar tragedy."

The interview ended, and the correspondent left, but Monks remained in his guarded room, having become a prisoner of city hall. His lot, though, compared favorably to the other men of the barkentine, held in the building's gloomy basement jail. Like Monks, none of them had been charged with any crime, but also like Monks, all were being detained at the insistence of Consul General Ingraham, who claimed US jurisdiction over the case, the three victims being American citizens and the *Herbert Fuller* being an American vessel that had departed from an American port.

Other than hold the men, though, Ingraham awaited word from Washington, DC, as to what else to do. While the consul general waited, he asked O'Sullivan that the prisoners in the basement not be permitted to communicate with each other. The chief complied but did allow reporters a few furtive interviews, and by talking to the prisoners, as well as working other leads, something of interest was gleaned by the press.

This was that certain astute Halifax wharf hands recognized Oscar Andersson from his days as a sailor on the steamers *Duart Castle* and *Barcelona*, not one year ago. At the time, according to the wharf hands, Andersson had been living in Halifax with a woman from Pictou, Nova Scotia, whom he may have also been married to, while also having a second woman in Saint John, New Brunswick. Then one day, these same wharf hands said, the Swedish vice consul in Halifax received letters from Andersson's wife back in Sweden inquiring of her husband's whereabouts, and it was soon thereafter that Andersson had departed for Boston. Other things, though, were learned by the press that might have some bearing on the crime.

For example, according to James Williams, the crusading secretary of the Atlantic Coast Seaman's Union, the *Herbert Fuller* had a reputation for being an unhappy ship. "Three years ago, Captain Nash landed at Wilmington, Delaware, from the West Indies, and charges of cruelty were proffered by his sailors," Williams said, adding that, "A year ago, the captain asked me to get a crew for him, but after trying six or seven days, I was obliged to give it up because the sailors had heard of him as being cruel."

In addition to this information, it had also been learned that the mate for the aborted voyage to Rosario, who on his shipping papers had identified himself as A. Thomas Bram of Bridgewater, Nova Scotia, turned out to be Thomas C. Bram or Thomas W. Bram or Thomas Mead Chambers Bram or Thomas Mead Chamberlain Bram of Saint Kitts, British West Indies. Whatever his exact name or origin, the word people used when describing Bram was *queer*.

"He was certainly a queer man," one of Bram's past employers, H. L. Joyce of the New York Lighter and Transportation Company, recalled, "and we who thought we knew him were being constantly surprised by him. When he came to us, it was with the strongest kind of reputation. I forget now whether he had been master or mate of a sailing vessel, but it was one or the other, and he was an unusually competent man, having led a seafaring life for many years."

Bram had been given command of the steam barge *Mystic* on Manhattan's East River, and Joyce said, "He was bright and intelligent and was scrupulously neat and well dressed—was, in fact, away above the average river man. He used to say he was a Nova Scotian, but we knew he was a half-bred Saint Kitts negro. He was very sensitive on this point, however, and the men on the river never had much to say when Bram got to talking about his nationality."

In fact, said Joyce, "Talking was Bram's greatest fault. He talked entirely too much for his own good. He was full of plans and schemes, and many people used to think he was demented."

One of Bram's schemes involved building a ship of his own that he could captain, and, despite the elaborate plans he had drawn up and improvements that he made to his plans on a daily basis, Bram became discouraged at not being able afford the ship's construction.

"Then he became money-mad," his former boss remembered, "and morning, noon, and night he talked nothing but money and his ship."

Bram had left Joyce's employ a year ago, June 1895, saying he had a yearning to go deep-sea sailing again and, shortly afterward, Joyce said, "His wife came to me and told me he had deserted her and her three children and that they were destitute. It was the third time he had done it, she said, and once before he had left her for three years, and she hadn't seen him at all during that time."

Bram's wife also told Joyce that she did not understand her husband at all, the man being never unkind to her when present and always buying little luxuries for her and the children. Then she hinted at a darker side to her husband, telling Joyce that, before he took off, he told her. "I may get into trouble one day, and if I do and you hear of it, be sure you don't talk too much, but notify my Masonic lodge, and they'll pull me through all right."

None of it made any sense to Joyce. "If he did this wholesale murdering he is accused of, he must have been insane. I have often suspected he might be slightly off, but I do not hesitate to say that had he come to me at any time before this affair, I would have given him his old position back."

Others also recalled Bram. One unnamed person, a former colleague of Bram's, remembered him as having been the day manager of the Dennett's restaurant on Boston's newspaper row eleven years before. The Dennett's chain, founded by "old man" Alfred W. Dennett, who later gave away his fortune to charity, was known for its fish cakes and beans but more so for its religiosity. At all Dennett's restaurants, verses from the Bible adorned the walls (along with signs warning patrons to be aware of pickpockets), and Bram had fit right in.

"Yes, I remember him perfectly," the former colleague said. "He had been a seafarer, then a waiter, and had just the qualities that led the old man to eventually put him in charge of the place. I remember he had a tremendously deep and powerful bass voice. In talking I can never forget that voice. He had the appearance of being an extraordinarily religious man, too, always entered fervently into the religious service, which is held in Dennett's for the employees every morning, and he could frequently be seen laboring earnestly with the waiters for their conversion."

The old man later had Bram manage a Dennett's in New York, but then, according to the former colleague, Bram struck out on his own and started a restaurant and bar, but that venture failed, and Bram returned to the sea.

"He looked like some kind of foreigner," the former colleague said. "Spanish or Portuguese or something, but I don't remember what nationality he claimed to be. He always seemed queer—I can't tell you just how, but he was queer."

All that, though, was in the past, and now in Halifax, and on the second day of Bram's stay in the city hall jail, Chief O'Sullivan turned him over to Detective Power (the same detective who, in 1883, foiled a

Fenian plot to dynamite the HMS *Canada*, which at the time had Prince—later King—George aboard).

Power said, "Come along with me," and took Bram to his office, where he ordered him to strip. Bram did as he was told, and then Power said, "Bram, we are trying to unravel this horrible mystery. Your position is rather an awkward one. I have had Brown in this office, and he made a statement that he saw you do the murder."

"He could not have seen me. Where was he?"

"He states he was at the wheel."

"Well, he could not see me from there."

"Now, look here, Bram. I am satisfied that you killed the captain from all I have heard from Mr. Brown. But, some of us here think you could not have done all that crime alone. If you had an accomplice, you should say so and not have the blame of this horrible crime on your own shoulders."

"Well, I think, and many others onboard the ship think, that Brown is the murderer, but I don't know anything about it."

Power then told Bram to put his clothes back on, all except for his suspenders and the inside lining of his white straw hat (the one with a hole in the crown), both of which Power kept. Power then brought Bram back to his cell, being perfectly satisfied with how the interview, brief though it was, had gone, especially Bram's damaging statement that the man at the wheel "could not see me from there."

That evening, a large crowd gathered at the entrance of the building, hoping for a glance of Franklin Monks and his brother, Dr. George Monks, and the crowd was not disappointed when the two appeared at ten fifty. Ironically, just before receiving Lester's telegram urging he come to Halifax, Franklin Monks had sent letters to Buenos Aires and Rosario hoping to catch his son in either place. In the letters to his son, Franklin confirmed what both already knew, that Lester would never return to Harvard, but also recommended that, from Argentina, Lester take a steamer to Liverpool and then spend a year in Europe with relatives before coming home. Now, however, Lester stood right before his father's teary eyes, and Europe could wait. After their emotional reunion, father and son were ready for a midnight conference with Chief O'Sullivan and also with Frank G. Forbes, a local attorney retained by the senior Monks to represent Lester in whatever official proceedings transpired. For the next hour, the quartet discussed the situation.

Legally, things stood like this: The Halifax stipendiary (a type of civil magistrate), George H. Fielding, had scheduled a hearing for eleven the next morning, Thursday, July 23. At that hearing the stipendiary would receive the city medical examiner's report and, by applying the local coroner's act, determine if murder had taken place aboard the *Herbert Fuller*. Certainly, the ruling would be in the affirmative, but the question remained if it would be Fielding for Halifax or Ingraham for the United States who would level charges of homicide against one or more of the nine detainees at city hall. As one of these detainees, and the only one who undisputedly had been inside the afterhouse at the time of the crime, Monks could possibly be implicated. To erase any such danger, therefore, out of tomorrow's hearing, attorney Forbes had to get nothing less than his client's total exoneration.

The Halifax medical examiner, Dr. William D. Finn, had autopsied the bodies the day they were landed in Halifax, and he arrived at city hall at ten forty-five the next morning with two copies of his report in hand. At autopsy, the doctor had found that the captain's wife was remarkably well preserved but that her husband and the second mate were in an appalling state of decay, in fact among the worst states of human decay he had ever seen. All three, Finn ruled, had been killed by a sharp instrument such as an ax, the skulls of the three victims having been crushed in and their faces torn open.

In addition to examining the victim's heads, Finn had removed their clothing but not after first noting that the wife's nightgown had been pushed up to her waist, leading him to surmise that she had been the victim of, he explained in his report, "attempted felonious assault."

Finn discovered that the captain's body below the neck showed no visible damage but that the second mate had clearly received several blows to his chest and, most horribly, the wife had obviously been struck on the hands, arms, and breasts. The wounds to her hands (her right hand hung from the wrist by just a strand of flesh) and arms were of particular interest to Finn, leading him to surmise that she had bravely attempted to ward off the first swings of the ax. In summary, Finn reckoned that the captain got seven blows to the head; the captain's wife, seven or eight to the head and body; and the second mate, another seven to the head and body.

In addition to the autopsies, Dr. Finn's report included findings from two separate visits to the afterhouse he had made that same day. The chart room, he saw, was in utter disarray, as if the captain had put up a ferocious struggle. The mattress and cot had been overturned, and books, papers, and other things had been tossed about in a chaotic manner. Finn also discovered gash marks on the heavy timbers of the chart room ceiling and also spots of red on the white ceiling paint, both undoubtedly being the result of an ax being repeatedly raised on the upswing.

However, the fact that the only sizable pool of blood in the room was located on the Brussels carpet right next to the cot where the captain had been sleeping (and the later finding at autopsy that the captain had suffered wounds only to the head), led Finn to conclude that the victim had no chance to resist but had been hacked mercilessly as he attempted to arise from his cot.

Moving to the second mate's stateroom, Finn had observed a gash to the top frame of the stateroom doorway, suggesting that the fiend had begun his devilish work with the ax while standing just outside in the forward companionway corridor. Within the tiny stateroom itself, Finn found that all was in disorder and that the bedding, originally a light color, had been dyed a dark red.

Finn had last examined the wife's stateroom, noting that both of its doors were unlocked, allowing the assassin entry from either the main cabin or from the passenger's stateroom. Compared to what Finn had just witnessed in the other two victims' rooms, the scene inside the wife's cabin was horrific. Here, gore stuck to a wall, covered much of the bedding, and had dripped down and soaked into the floor. On the bed were numerous locks of the victim's dark brown hair, leading the police to theorize that they had been sheared from her head by the same ax that had ended her life. But no, Finn ruled upon closer inspection, the locks had been cut by scissors in the normal fashion (but how they ended up on her bed, Finn did not say).

Although the wife's clothing was strewn about the room, and although at autopsy Finn found indications that she had tried to defend herself, Finn ultimately did not believe much of a struggle had taken place. Rather, the poor woman had been quickly hacked to death. And because the wife's wedding ring was in plain sight on top of her stateroom table, Finn also believed that, while he could not rule out "feloni-ous assault," robbery was probably not the killer's motive.

In terms of the sequence of the slaughter, Finn deduced that the captain was struck first, that the second mate was immediately struck next, and that the wife was struck last, as her screams would have logically awoken her husband and the second mate and that these two strong, seafaring men would have instantly leapt to her aid.

On the day of Stipendiary Fielding's inquest, Dr. Finn's report was still sealed and not for public consumption; but it was to see the men of the *Herbert Fuller* being arraigned in the police courtroom that the people wanted, and a throng numbering more than 1,600 formed a line from the entrance of city hall to the opposite side of Duke Street. Not all would gain entry, but those who did created such a rush for the courtroom that, in the confusion, two heavy desks were overturned, both of the courtroom's heavy doors were wrenched off their hinges, and twice the police had to restore order. The *Herbert Fuller*'s passen-ger, mate, and the rest were expected to make their entry soon, but in a bitter disappointment to the spectators, some of whom had already perched themselves on windowsills for a better view, O'Sullivan an-nounced that the hearing had been postponed. This had occurred, the chief said, so that Consul General Ingraham could hold his tribunal first, which was now taking place somewhere in the building, the exact location the chief refused to reveal.

City hall, however, had only so many rooms, and word quickly spread that Ingraham's tribunal was being held in the magistrate's of-fice. O'Sullivan, though, beat the crowd there and stubbornly guarded the door such that neither members of the public nor the press were permitted even so much as a peek inside. Had they been allowed to, they would have witnessed an exclusive gathering consisting of Franklin and Lester Monks, Frank Forbes, John Snow, Wilber Nash, and Darius Ingraham.

Present to lend a hand were a stenographer and William F. MacCoy, the Halifax city recorder, who administered the tribunal on Ingraham's behalf. MacCoy first called Lester Monks, who had barely escaped being crushed by the horde in the corridor. The young fellow once again told his story, only this time his narrative, as expertly guided by Forbes, had none of the boastfulness or disjointedness displayed in his newspaper interview. Monks acquitted himself well, although in fact he had never been in jeopardy, the sole purpose of the tribunal being to gather evidence against the mate, who was now called into the magistrate's office.

Once inside, Bram answered the questions put to him but then faced a fierce cross-examination from Forbes who, with MacCoy and Ingraham making no objection and with young Monks being allowed to remain in the room, assumed the role of prosecutor. Although having no legal counsel of his own, Bram withstood the assault by the private attorney and, according to later reports, "clung" to his story that he had nothing to do with the murders. After Forbes had finished with Bram, the crowd of onlookers outside the doors parted as a special guard led the guilty one, described as being a "dark" and a "most powerful looking man" who had "certainly a bad looking face," back down to his cell.

Spencer was next, and with a policeman at his side to nudge him should he wander off script, Spencer confirmed everything Monks had earlier testified to, and then Brown was called in.

The forty-year-old sailor appeared every bit the Nordic mariner. When describing Brown one reporter later wrote:

> He is a native of Sweden, and is a representative specimen of the seamen of that country. He is not tall. His complexion is light, and he wears a sandy mustache and a beard a month old. Brown is a sturdy fellow, without the least hint of anything deceptive in his make-up. He might make a strong wrestler, but he never could wield a fencing foil. His English is decidedly broken, but he speaks so simply he has no trouble making himself understood. He is not, however, a man of ideas, and is not a success as a conversationalist.

The sailor would be, however, a success as a witness and made his debut that day in front of Ingraham's tribunal.

Brown testified that he had left Sweden in 1885 at age thirty after his parents died. He shipped as a seaman on the *Marie Russell* and then the *Bertie Biglow* and then scores of other vessels that brought him all over the world, but he lost contact with his brothers and sisters back home. On Christmas Day of last year, Brown said, he departed Calcutta as mate of the *Andrano* and arrived in Boston six months later, May 29. He took a room in a house on Commercial Street, where he worked for his board and lodging and then, five weeks later, signed with Captain Nash as a deckhand on the *Herbert Fuller*. Brown confirmed that he had never met the captain or any of the barkentine's other men before and that he took the mate, Bram, to be Italian. In terms of how everyone got along, Brown reported all got along fine, except for the two mates, Bram and Blomberg, who had had their differences.

Then Brown got to the heart of the matter. He stated that, on the morning of the murders, he was standing on the stern deck behind the afterhouse between twelve o'clock midnight and two o'clock in the morning, it being his trick at the wheel, when sometime after one o'clock he spied Bram descending into the afterhouse by the forward companionway. A short while later, Brown said he heard sounds coming from within.

Startled, Brown said he leaned way over to his right to where a small window, its curtain drawn back, looked into the chart room. He peered through the window and, even though the chart room lamp had gone out, said he could see Bram bring an ax down on Captain Nash as Nash lay on his cot. Next, Brown said he heard the captain's wife scream twice and knew that she, too, had been dealt with. Brown said he then saw Bram bound out of the forward companionway and come over the afterhouse roof toward him. Brown said he feared for his life and was paralyzed by fright. Smelling of whiskey but now without the ax, Bram, however, merely inquired as to how the ship was sailing.

After Brown was excused, the other men were led into the magistrate's office to give their testimony, but none had much to add because, at the time of the crime, all were either on watch forward or down in the forecastle and had been oblivious to the murders. Loheac, though, did recall that, a few days before the murders, Brown had told him he once shot a man in the head but was found insane and escaped prosecution. Brown, however, was not on trial here, and by five o'clock the consul general had gathered enough evidence to declare the inquisition over.

Ingraham had testimony from each of the nine witnesses typed up as depositions. (Forbes carefully reviewed the one based on Monks's testimony before allowing his client to sign it.) Ingraham also filed a typewritten report, running fifty large pages, greatly damning of Bram. However, the formalities of having the accused charged with the crime had already been taken care of because, that morning, and before his hearing had even started, Ingraham demanded that the Halifax city clerk issue a warrant charging the mate with triple murder.

In advance of the next week's annual carnival, Halifax teemed with vacationers, and the many Americans among them were disgusted by Ingraham's star chamber proceedings, so at odds with their understanding of what should be judicial openness and fairness. The inquiry held by Stipendiary Fielding the following day, Friday, July 24, did nothing to allay the criticism; it, too, was conducted behind closed doors and served no purpose other than to condemn Bram, which it did.

Normally, the stipendiary's ruling would have paved the way for a Halifax trial, but as Ingraham made clear, Bram would instead face charges in Boston and would remain in custody until that time. The steward and the six sailors were also to remain in custody because their testimony would be needed at trial.

Testimony from the former passenger Monks would be required, too, but the consul general announced at the conclusion of Fielding's hearing that the young man would be released into the custody of his father. Soon father and son could be seen together trotting around the city in a carriage, dining at the Queen Hotel, or walking the paths of the public gardens.

Spencer learned of the special consideration Monks had received and was outraged. Why, Spencer demanded of a newspaper reporter, should Monks go free while he had to stay locked up in a four-foot-by-seven-foot prison cell, sleep on a wooden plank, and only with difficulty be permitted to send a message to his pregnant wife in New York informing her of his whereabouts? As for the navigational skills Monks claimed to have had, Spencer told the same reporter that those claims were "all rot"; that neither he nor the passenger "knew anything about navigation"; that they had been "hopelessly adrift" when found by the Halifax pilots; and that, if not for the earlier directions given by the fisherman, "we would have gone ashore."

In a highly irritable mood and for a moment neglected by his police handlers, Spencer also lit into Brown: "That man's an awful liar! You can't believe a word he says. He knows more about the murder than he wanted to tell at first, and he hasn't told it all yet. It's all between himself and that mate Bram. If they would only tell, they would give the whole story, but they want to lie about it. He stands there, telling you a long story about himself that you can't believe. I wouldn't believe him on my oath. Don't you listen to him! He's a liar! Why didn't he at first tell what he saw? He's lying now, and he's been lying all along."

After having played host to his jailhouse guests for nearly a week, and also needing his officers for carnival, O'Sullivan wanted the *Fuller* men shipped off to Boston forthwith. Ingraham wanted this, too, and had secretly booked berths aboard the Plant Line steamer *Halifax*. Knowing or suspecting this, on Saturday the chief had a boat take Monks and Spencer out to the *Herbert Fuller*, Monks to gather his many possessions and Spencer to help look for a gold watch belonging to Captain Nash and a gold ring belonging to Mrs. Nash (Spencer could find neither). The boat returned with the passenger's luggage and other personal effects and also with the crew's belongings. At nine o'clock that evening, the crew's things were deposited at the police station in city hall and ready for the men to claim.

Bram laid claim to some whiskey he had brought aboard the barkentine but, knowing he would not be allowed liquor anytime soon, gave it to O'Sullivan. Missing, however, was Bram's trunk, which did not arrive until an hour later, and when it did it was obvious that it had been crudely pried open and then just as crudely nailed shut. The trunk was unnailed, and Bram was allowed to change into clean underwear, a shirt, a tie, and a heavy three-piece suit (perhaps packed earlier in anticipation of the Argentinian winter).

Later that same evening, all was in readiness for departure. The city hall inmates had signed away their rights to fight extradition. O'Sullivan had appointed one of his constables to accompany the men on their journey, and Ingraham had tried to keep the timing of departure, at two o'clock Sunday morning, secret by misleading the press and the public. However, Ingraham had done so in vain because a score of reporters and a crowd of hundreds gathered around city hall at midnight to see the men of the *Herbert Fuller*, especially that murderer Thomas Bram, off for Boston. All the men, except for Monks, who was allowed to freely board the *Halifax* at his leisure, were hustled out of city hall with their wrists clasped in irons and packed into hackneys for the short ride to the Plant Line Wharf. Once onboard the steamer, the captives were shown to their assigned berths. Bram and Brown were confined to two separate cabins, while the steward and the six sailors were locked in a single room. Meanwhile the Monks party, consisting of Lester, Franklin, George, and legal counsel Forbes, had the run of the ship.

From now on the citizens of Halifax would have to get their news of the murders from the Boston States (as they called the nation to their south) but not before the sailor Brown, in his jail cell before departure, claimed that he was Dutch and his real name was Johese Vastbac. Curious, a Halifax reporter asked him why had he concealed this. The sailor explained that he once got into trouble with a captain and later that captain had been after him, so had to assume a new identity.

This was quickly confirmed by an unnamed acquaintance in Boston.

"Vastbac, or Brown, is a native of Holland," this person told a reporter from the *Globe*, "and at one time sailed as first mate from the ports of that country. He is a good, reliable, and willing worker and decidedly industrious and sober when he is on the high seas."

The acquaintance added, however, "He has what the boys call 'wheels in the head' and often does strange things. He is constantly talking and mumbling to himself and sometimes entertains fears that some unknown persons are following him with the intention of injuring him bodily. When he drinks to excess, he becomes crazed and is almost uncontrollable. While in his old age he may be harmless, he has figured on one or two unpleasant occurrences during his life aboard ship. He shot at a mate in one of his crazy spells. At that time he believed the man was following him to kill him. I believe this happened in Holland."

The acquaintance cautioned, "He will not talk of himself at any length, so it is impossible to get at the facts. I don't think the old man has a friend or relative in the world outside the few he has made among his fellow seamen. When he shipped on the *Herbert Fuller*, he expressed a doubt about going in her. He said, 'I don't like the look of that fellow's face. I am afraid he is a rough man to get along with. I never did like a nigger for a boss, and I'm afraid that cuss Bram will make trouble for some of us before we get to port.'"

The acquaintance concluded of Brown, "It took some little persuasion to finally induce the old man to sail with the 'half-breed,' as he called Mate Bram."

When the *Halifax* steamed out of the harbor in the early morning of Sunday, July 26, it passed the dark silhouette of a forlorn barkentine at anchor with a partly submerged (for purification purposes) jolly boat floating off its stern. The horror ship had become the subject of dispute between John Swann, who had hired a new captain and crew and wanted the *Herbert Fuller* and its cargo of white pine sailed to Rosario without delay, and the US district attorney in Boston, who wanted the vessel in that city to serve as an exhibit in the upcoming murder trial.

While Swann stayed in Halifax to protect his floating assets, Wilber Nash had already left by train for Maine. The bodies of his brother and sister-in-law, hermetically sealed in two coffins, would follow on a later train.

The funeral took place on the same Saturday that the nine living souls from the *Herbert Fuller* were preparing to depart Halifax for Boston. In the little village of Harrington, Maine, businesses had closed by twelve noon, and the blueberry fields for miles around were empty of their usual pickers. All that morning carriages loaded with mourners had rumbled in from outlying farms, and by the time of the service, the pews of the Baptist church were so packed that extra chairs had to be found to accommodate those without a seat. The four surviving Nash brothers, men of iron nerve, dissolved into tears, as did every other person present. The Reverend Selden Gilbert quoted from Longfellow's sonnet to Michael Angelo:

> Nothing that is shall perish utterly,
> But perish only to revive again
> In other forms, as clouds restore in rain
> The exhalations of the land and sea.

Then, for the next thirty minutes, the reverend delivered a sermon that helped dry the eyes of the weeping congregants. The weather, which until then had been overcast and rainy, gave way to a blazing sunshine as the procession walked to the cemetery, the coffins borne by sixteen pallbearers, many of them master mariners who, from the little village of Harrington, had literally sailed the seven seas. Charles and Laura were buried next to each other beneath a Norway pine, now shipmates for all eternity.

A far humbler service had taken place four days earlier at the Camp Hill Cemetery in Halifax. There, in the presence of a clergyman and a knot of onlookers, the *Herbert Fuller*'s second mate was buried in that section of the graveyard reserved for those with no known friends or family.

CHAPTER 5

As the sun rose on Monday morning, July 27, the *Halifax* tied up at Lewis Wharf after steaming west for thirty hours. Thousands of Bostonians had gathered in hopes of seeing the actors in a drama that until now they had only read about. And sure enough, there the actors were, all the *Fuller* men visible on deck except for the "boy-hero," as the newspapers had dubbed him, Lester Monks. Unbeknownst to the crowd, Monks remained in his cabin to confer with prominent Boston attorney Alfred Hemenway, who had just come aboard. A phalanx of Boston blue shirts had also just come aboard to escort all but the missing Monks down the gangway.

Bram and Brown both appeared in fine spirits, especially Brown, who laughed and exchanged fond farewells with the ship's officers. When Bram stepped onto the wharf, the crowd could see that he was manacled, unshaven, and a little disheveled but also surprisingly overdressed for a summer's day, wearing a derby hat, heavy winter overcoat, and gray trousers. At the dock the prisoners were questioned by immigration officers Skeffington and Toland, and the nearest onlookers could hear Bram calmly stating that he was thirty-three years of age, had been born in Ireland under the British flag, weighed 158 pounds, and was married. The onlookers could also see that Bram, with his dark complexion made even darker by a sunburned face, looked distinctly Cuban.

The shackled men were put in a patrol wagon and, trailed by a large crowd, driven to Police Station 1, where they were stuffed into holding cells. Monks, appearing refreshed and wearing a straw hat and nattily attired in a summer suit, walked to the station on his own accord. In the station captain's private office, the young man was soon enjoying breakfast with his father, Franklin; his uncle George; and his Halifax lawyer, Forbes. He also conferred once again with Hemenway and greeted some chums who had come to the station to welcome him home. Later that morning, Monks and the rest of the *Fuller* men were taken to a courtroom within the enormous post office at Post Office Square, which doubled as the city's federal building. There Bram and Brown were arraigned on multiple counts of murder.

For Bram, the charges must have been expected, but for Brown, having been Ingraham's star witness in Halifax, they were shocking indeed, and when he heard them, he could only mutter that, while he "had seen most of it," he had not done the killings. The two accused were ordered jailed without bail, while the other six men, accused of nothing at all, were ordered held in lieu of one hundred dollars bail as witnesses. Monks, of course, was immediately released on his own recognizance and, returning to the family mansion in suburban Longwood, had the pleasure that night of sleeping in his own bed. In contrast, the other witnesses did not make bail and, like the prisoners Bram and Brown, spent their night in the Charles Street Jail, a magnificent edifice of granite yet having none of the comforts of home.

This grossly unequal treatment again grated on the steward, and during a break in the legal proceedings the previous morning he had lashed out at the privileged passenger.

"I do not think it is fair for people to make so much about Monks navigating the ship into Halifax," Spencer told a *Boston Herald* reporter. "All I have got to thank him for is that he loaned me his revolver. With that in my possession, I was able to do a good deal. Monks had never been onboard a ship before, and he was sick before he came onboard and seasick after we got outside [Boston Harbor]."

Referring to the discovery of the captain's body, Spencer added, "The great wonder is that he was able to compose himself at all when he met the mate after leaving the cabin. He had to go through the cabin where the bodies were; he could not help it, but he was afraid to notify me because the mate would not go forward with him."

Spencer also continued with the theory he had begun to advance a few days earlier in Halifax, which was that Bram had not acted alone and that Brown's version of events could not be trusted.

"There are some things that will have to be explained in connection with Bram and Brown to show that both did not know what was going to happen," Spencer insisted.

The next morning, the *Fuller* men again found themselves in the federal building courtroom. There they were met by a throng of spectators and also by the US commissioner for Boston, a man named Fiske, who would preside over the hearing. When seated, Monks had both his Halifax attorney, Forbes, and his Boston attorney, Hemenway, at his side, but for the first time, Bram also had legal counsel. This was James Edward Cotter, retained by two anonymous Boston businessmen (rumored to be the principals of Shepard & Morse, owners of the barkentine's white pine) who had known Bram for some years and wanted to ensure that he got a fair hearing.

Cotter wasted no time by defending Bram and instead informed Fiske that he knew practically nothing about the case and asked that the hearing be postponed until Friday. Bram's codefendant, Brown, still lacked an attorney, and this fact, in addition to Cotter's request, convinced Fiske to grant the delay.

That Friday the courtroom was so jammed with the curious that they impeded the proceedings, and those without seats had to be shown the door. Frank Loheac testified first, followed by Monks. After listening to the young man's harrowing tale, Cotter rose to ask if he "agreed now" that the mate's recommendation to take a steamer to South America instead of the barkentine "was pretty good advice?"

"Yes, sir," Monks answered.

No other witnesses took the stand, but Brown's new attorney, Frank D. Allen, was given the opportunity to address the court: "If there is anything on which to hold Brown, then there is equally strong ground on which to hold this young man Monks."

He then added that to accuse Monks would, of course, be "preposterous, your honor, but not one whit more than to suggest that Charley Brown committed this crime."

Commissioner Fiske disagreed and ruled that there was "probable cause" to hold both Bram and Brown until the two defendants could be brought before the final session of the grand jury of the US Circuit

Court for the District of Massachusetts, scheduled for October. Fiske also increased bail for the jailed witnesses to five hundred dollars, all but ensuring their confinement until then.

The "plucky cook," as Spencer's growing number of admirers called him, would normally have taken this news hard, but he had already gained his freedom. It so happened that a wealthy and philanthropic Bostonian, Dr. John Dixwell, had previously attempted to free Spencer by soliciting the help of Franklin Monks. The doctor had wired Franklin in Halifax, explaining that he would furnish bail "to the Canadian authorities in any amount" such that "this poor colored man" be given the "same privileges as had already been accorded to" Franklin's son Lester.

The doctor was never favored by a reply, but in Boston his efforts proved more successful. Thanks to the doctor's largess, the steward, after several nights spent in the Charles Street Jail, had been freed on a one-thousand-dollar bond. Now at liberty to pursue demands for salvage rights to the *Herbert Fuller* and its cargo, Spencer retained a Boston attorney to press his claim and then took a train down to New York. Among his first stops seems to have been a lodging house in Brooklyn.

On the front steps of the lodging house was Bram's wife, a woman of German descent named Nettie, and their three young children. While the children remained outside, the adults, including an unnamed *New York Times* reporter, went inside, where Spencer informed Nettie that the man she had married and whom she (Spencer assumed) thought was white was actually a "negro."

Thomas Bram, Spencer said, had deceived her, adding that, prior to their marriage, his associations had all been with people of a different color from her own. Nettie took the news in silence and then plaintively asked if her husband in the year since abandoning her and the children had ever been in New York. Wishing to hide nothing, Spencer replied yes, her husband had been in New York for an athletic event, where he had taken a dozen people to dinner.

Leaving the forlorn woman to her misery, Spencer left the lodging house and outside told the reporter that Bram was very sensitive about the "color question." Shortly after they first met, Spencer explained, Bram had asked him, "Steward, you would not blame a man for passing off as a white man if he could do it?"

"No," Spencer said he had answered.

"You see, there is such a prejudice against the colored man that he cannot get a show, and if he could fool people, I think he is perfectly justified in doing so."

Back in Boston, Bram sang hymns in his jail cell and impressed visitors with his piety, and north of Boston in Gloucester, a mariner named Frank Gnirke recalled a voyage he had taken with Bram more than a decade ago.

"In the year 1883," Gnirke told an inquiring reporter, "I shipped aboard the schooner *Lucy Hastings* of Bangor, Maine, for Tampico, Mexico. Thomas Bram, who said he was born in Saint Kitts, was shipped as mate. The first time we saw him, he drove to the pier where the schooner was lying. He came in great style, accompanied by his wife and driven by a coachman. At first we thought he was the owner of the cargo, until we found out to the contrary. He was dressed in fine shape."

The master of the schooner was a Captain Gray, and at first he thought highly of Bram, but according to Gnirke, the sailors thought otherwise, finding the new mate to be very "gullible, ready to believe almost anything they told him, no matter how absurd."

Gnirke added of Bram, "He had a mania for becoming the owner and master of a ship. That was a continuous topic of his conversation, and he had plans of the brig that he was going to build, which he showed on many occasions, stating that his wife's relatives were rich and would build the ship for him. The building of this vessel seemed to be the height of his ambition. He referred to it time and time again. He said he was born in Saint Kitts, and although the subject was never alluded to in his presence, it was evident he had negro blood in him. His wife, he stated, was of German origin."

During the sail to Mexico, Gnirke remembered, the "best of feeling prevailed" onboard ship, with the "good-natured and jolly" mate being "soft" on the crew.

"As an illustration of his character," Gnirke said of Bram, "an incident may be related that occurred while the vessel was lying off Tampico bar, before proceeding up the harbor. The captain had gone ashore, and the men commenced to get impatient to get to the city, saying that the captain was having a good time and they ought to be enjoying themselves. In the cargo were about fifty barrels of lager. Some of the crew suggested that Bram break into the barrels so they could all have a drink. To the surprise of the men, he fell in with the suggestion."

Gnirke continued, "It was with great difficulty that the barrels were reached, as they were stowed in the bottom of the hold. But several were secured and broken open and the beer taken and consumed. In putting the barrels back, it was found impossible to replace some of the cargo, so it was thrown overboard, amounting to a value of about one hundred dollars. After the schooner got to Tampico, Bram was ashore every night and showed a decided preference for women. It was his conduct while in port that led Captain Gray to revise his opinion of the mate."

When not carousing, Bram sang hymns, and he had a very good voice.

"He apparently knew all the hymns in the book," Gnirke recalled. "He would go ashore while at Tampico with some of the crew and would sing for hours on the plaza."

"While still in port," Gnirke added, "one of the seamen, Frank Cohorst, was accidently drowned by the overturning of the boat by the strong current, it being then in the rainy season, when the water was running high. Captain Gray was very much affected, as were the crew, but Bram showed not the slightest concern, and the men put him down as unfeeling. When he left Tampico, he took five or six cases of gin. He was very liberal with it on the passage to New York, treating the men liberally. While on the passage he had an altercation with a young man, a passenger named Stevens. One night the passenger was steering, and Bram found fault with his work, saying that he did not steer straight. Some words resulted, at which Bram hauled off and struck Stevens. Although the latter was a man of light build, he sailed into Bram, the result being that a scrape followed, in which Stevens got the best of the argument."

"On the passage home, while he was under the weather," Gnirke continued of Bram, "the sailors took occasion of his gullibility to play practical jokes [on] him. He would take anything they would recommend and fix up as decoctions of tar, water, et cetera, which he swallowed without question."

Changing the subject, Gnirke then said of Bram, "He seemed to think a great deal of his wife and frequently referred to her, speaking of her in the highest terms. She was evidently a conscientious woman."

The *Hastings* docked in New York, where Bram was paid off before proceeding to Haverhill, Massachusetts, with a load of coal. There, the captain called the crew and said, "I now know where the beer went to; you fellows drank it up."

It transpired that that the captain had received a letter from Bram's wife with a check for the amount of beer and property destroyed.

Gnirke continued, "The impression I got of Bram was that he was rather cowardly and the last man whom I would think of committing murder. In fact, I should not be afraid to face him, even with an ax in his hand. I could never imagine he could muster up courage enough to do such a deed."

Gnirke added, though, that "if he committed the deed aboard the *Fuller*, then, in my opinion, he did it to carry out his cherished ambition of becoming owner and master of a ship, for which he had a perfect mania. It was the consuming ambition of his life."

Another mariner, a first-class seaman named Johnny Ostergren of the US survey schooner *Eagre*, also recalled a past voyage, only this one was with Charles Nash.

"I shipped on the barkentine *Herbert Fuller*, September 30, 1891, and left her on her return to New York, April 23, 1892," he told a news correspondent. "The experiences of that trip made me determined never to sail with Captain Nash again."

Ostergren explained, "Never before have I known men to be worked so hard on a vessel as on that voyage, and if my experience isn't enough, the statements of the men who were members of the crew with me will show the same thing. We were pushed just as far as the law allowed on our work. For instance, where ordinarily ships' captains allow the day watches four hours off and four on, we were compelled every day to give the whole day to watch and allowed no layoff, and night after night, the watch below was called out to work the ship when the weather was almost absolutely calm."

Ostergren added, "We were ready to turn out when occasion required, but when, it seemed to us after repeated occurrences, that the captain was doing it for his own pleasure—we could figure out no other reason—the thing got very monotonous."

After crossing the Atlantic, the *Herbert Fuller* docked at Cardiff, Wales, where all the sailors except for Ostergren vanished. The men had signed with Nash twenty-two days earlier at twenty-five dollars a month, and as an advance Nash gave each thirty dollars, so by fleeing the vessel the sailors had not only deserted their captain but also cheated him. Yet there were no complaints coming from Nash, Ostergren explained, because the going wage for a sailor in Cardiff was just seventeen dollars and fifty cents a month, so by hiring a replacement crew in Cardiff, Nash had made out nicely.

The next stop on the voyage was Pernambuco, Brazil, but Ostergren remembered, "We were not allowed shore liberty, although the crews of every other vessel in that place, of all nations, were given that privilege. The only time I got on shore was Sunday mornings, when the captain would take me with him to carry on my back the provisions he purchased in the town."

The second mate was a man named Biger Muchino, and one day Muchino snuck ashore and got drunk.

"When he returned," Ostergren said, "the captain took him down into his cabin and thumped him unmercifully. Of course, nothing could be done about this, as there were no witnesses, but the appearance of the mate after he came from the cabin was proof enough that he had been punched, and punched hard."

A few days later, Nash wanted to go up to the town and had Muchino row him in a dinghy to a wharf. He told Muchino to let him off but not to tie up. Six hours later Nash returned and was irate.

"It happened that the heavy swell forced the dinghy against the landing and scratched off some of the paint," Ostergren said. "The captain saw this and asked the mate if he had been ashore. The answer was that he had but only for about five minutes to get a drink of water. The captain called him a liar and said he knew better, and after some words on the way out to the vessel, he also called the mate a very insulting name. Muchino was a much smaller man than the captain, but as they jumped aboard he said he would fight Captain Nash if the latter would fight fair. The captain said he would fight fair and told the mate to go to the cabin. The mate replied that he would not go there and get punched as he had been before but would fight fair on the deck. The captain repeated his command, and the mate again refused, saying he was not going to be abused."

According to Ostergren, Captain Nash then called for Mrs. Nash, and crying, she appeared on deck.

"Get me my biggest revolver," the captain demanded.

"You don't want your revolver," she pleaded but then did as ordered.

Holding his biggest revolver and standing in front of Muchino, who according to Ostergren did not flinch, the captain said, "Now you can see I can shoot you."

"Go ahead," said Muchino.

The captain fired. The bullet just grazed the mate's head and went tearing through the cabin and settled in a bulkhead. The captain did not fire again, and the matter stopped there.

Ostegren related, "Afterward the men were good friends, although the mate never forgot the matter and often referred to it."

When the voyage finally ended back in New York, Ostergren stated, "Every man was glad to get out of the craft. None of them ever shipped again, and I do not believe they could have been induced to go with Captain Nash on a second voyage. I know I could not."

Ostergren was also familiar with another incident concerning the captain (the one that got the attention of Williams of the Seaman's Union). This one occurred in 1893, when, Ostergren explained, the crew after a long voyage aboard the *Herbert Fuller* refused to sail the vessel from the Delaware Breakwater and demanded to be let off at Wilmington, charging Nash with cruelty. Nash at first stood firm but then relented and allowed his men to be landed in Wilmington (where, of course, they were duly jailed for insubordination). Although he was ultimately victorious, the incident, Ostergren explained, had earned Nash a certain degree of notoriety among maritime folk up and down the East Coast.

CHAPTER 6

The *Herbert Fuller* slipped out of Halifax Harbor at daybreak, August 17. The elopement caught Spencer's attorney by surprise, and now with the vessel and its cargo gone, so too were his client's hopes for salvage rights. Ingraham (caring nothing about the colored steward's salvage or any other rights) had permitted the departure by accepting John Swann's specious argument that, because the afterhouse had been scrubbed clean since the murders, the vessel could never serve as evidence against the accused.

In Boston two months later, October 20, a grand jury was seated in a federal building courtroom, and being a grand jury, its subsequent proceedings were and remain a secret. Reporters who were milling about, however, spied young Monks in the US district attorney's office and assumed he would testify, and while they did not see him, they also believed Spencer had returned from New York and would do likewise. The reporters could confirm, however, that three new witnesses would appear before the grand jury. Two of these, Herman Schiewe and Peter West, first and second mates, respectively, of the vessel *Rocky Glen*, apparently possessed information of immense interest and had been summoned to tell what they knew. The third new witness was a stevedore named Francis C. Stevens, who, while caulking the *Herbert Fuller* before it left Boston, had apparently overhead something of great importance. (Whatever it was that Schiewe, West, and Stevens had to offer, however, could not have been much because none of the three subsequently testified at trial.)

The grand jury reconvened the next day and heard from the defendant Brown and also from some of the sailors but did not, and would never, hear from the other defendant, Bram, who was not invited to tell his side of the story. The jurors concluded their secret work, and two weeks later their decision was unsealed. Brown had not been indicted for anything, but Bram had to stand silently as the court clerk read twenty minutes' worth of formal charges against him. When done with his reading, the clerk asked Bram, "Prisoner, what say you to this indictment?"

"Not guilty."

"How will you be tried?" the clerk continued. "By God and by country?"

"Yes sir."

Wishing the defendant luck by quoting Erasmus, as was the courtroom custom at the time, the clerk declared, "God send you a good delivery."

Present in the courtroom and still representing the accused was James Cotter. Because his client had been declared indigent, the US district attorney's office would have to reimburse him for expenses, but not for his time, of which he gave without compensation. However, even if Bram had the means to hire and lavishly pay anyone of his choice, he could have done no better than—as the press warily called Cotter—the "lynx-eyed counselor."

Born in Ireland, Cotter had immigrated at age seven after his mother died and was raised on his father's farm in Marlboro outside of Boston. He attended public schools and for higher education went to Bridgewater State Normal School, a teacher's college. Cotter's knowledge of the law came not from any classroom but from working in a Marlboro attorney's office, and now at age forty-eight, Cotter had been chief counsel in several famous cases. Most sensationally, he had successfully defended Joseph Welch, blamed for the Old Colony Railroad disaster that killed sixteen passengers, and also Anna M. Makepeace, charged in the shooting death of Clarence E. Makepeace, her abusive husband.

For his newest challenge, that of saving Bram's neck from the hangman's noose, Cotter was assisted by his junior counsel. This was a promising young attorney named Asa Palmer French of the noted French family of Braintree, Massachusetts. French had been educated at Thayer, Yale, and Boston University Law School.

The upcoming trial brought back memories of the last federal murder case Boston had witnessed. This was in 1888, when Captain Marcus C. Howes of the bark *Freeman* stood accused of shooting and killing Idako Kikumatsu on the high seas. In his defense, the captain explained that the "Jap" sailor had been averse to bathing and, when told to take one on the morning of the shooting, had spoken back "snappishly." The captain said he responded by hitting the sailor twice with a belaying pin. Then, around six o'clock that evening, the captain saw the sailor and ordered him "to mind your business and don't bother me."

The sailor made a profane reply, and the captain punched him in the face. Enraged, the sailor grappled with the captain and tried to throw him overboard before fleeing to the forecastle. From inside the forecastle the steward told the captain, "He is here and will not come out," and the captain replied, "Go and bring me my revolver."

Twice the captain gave the sailor the opportunity to come out on deck.

"Come in here," the sailor had replied both times.

When the captain finally did, the sailor approached him while holding, the captain claimed, a weapon of some sort. The captain fired, and the sailor died a half hour later.

There the matter would normally have ended, but it was Howes's misfortune that the Japanese government learned of the killing and demanded justice. At trial various facts unfavorable to the captain emerged. Among these were that Howes was known to be of a quarrelsome nature, that he had been drinking gin throughout the day of the killing, and that the weapon Kikumatsu supposedly had when Howes shot him was never found. The jury rejected a verdict of murder but did find Howes guilty of manslaughter.

US Circuit Court Judge LeBaron Bradford Colt of Rhode Island had presided over that trial, and along with US District Court Judge Nathan Webb of Maine, he would preside over this trial, too. Prosecuting the case would be the US attorney for the district of Massachusetts and a former US congressman, Sherman Hoar. Thirty-six years old, Hoar was the scion of a prominent Concord family (his great-grandfather had signed both the Declaration of Independence and the Constitution) and the son of Judge E. Rockwood Hoar (whose eloquent instructions given to a jury in 1851 are still quoted in jurors' handbooks today).

Sherman Hoar was a graduate of Phillips Exeter, Harvard, and Harvard Law. He had a sharp mind to match his orator's voice, and his head was so quintessentially "Puritan" (as defined in the late nineteenth century) that the sculptor Daniel Chester French, a family friend, used him as a model for the statue of John Harvard that now sits in Harvard Yard.

Due to an error in the grand jury's indictment, the government was limited to charging Bram with just a single count of murder, and so Hoar chose to try him for that of Charles Nash, the only one to which there was an alleged witness. (To foster his case, however, Hoar fully intended to implicate Bram in the other two murders.)

The trial, *United States, by indictment, v. Thomas Bram, alias*, commenced in mid-December and like the pretrial hearings was held in a courtroom within the federal building (spectators as usual clogging the corridors).

On the first day Bram, dressed in a white bow tie and a black suit, with a Freemason badge pinned to the coat lapel, sat seated in the prisoner's dock, his hands temporarily freed of manacles. The accused listened intently as the proceedings got under way, as did the twelve jurors seated in the jury box who would decide whether he lived or died.

The twelve jurors were "ordinary men," as the *Globe* described them, who hailed from all corners of the commonwealth. For example, the jury foreman, Rinaldo A. Jack, was a traveling salesman from East Boston, Charles A. Howes was a sailmaker from Chatham, Henry J. Arnold worked in lumber and was from Adams, and Shepard R. Dyer was a farmer from Plainfield. And of course being "ordinary men," as that term was understood in 1896, meant that all twelve were white.

Hoar's assistant US district attorneys, John H. Casey and Frederick P. Cabot, had been expected to do the actual courtroom work, but in a move that took legal observers by surprise, apparently Hoar would do this himself. Arising from his chair and standing to his full height, the district attorney began his lengthy opening argument: "Gentleman of the jury. . . . At midnight on the fourteenth day of July, hundreds of miles from land, the barkentine *Herbert Fuller* was sailing on the high seas. At two o'clock in the morning, of the twelve persons who were on the vessel at midnight, three had been murdered. No human being could have reached her except those onboard. Within the limits and walls of that American vessel, you must hunt for the man who did these murders. . . . I need not impress upon you the necessity of weighing with the greatest care everything which is presented to you in the trial of the case. Here is human life hanging in the balance, and the law surrounds that human life with every protection imaginable. I should do my duty poorly if I tried to create any prejudice against the man in the dock. But I should fail in my duty if I did not impress upon your minds that your verdict will be the means of protecting the men who sail under the American flag all over the world."

When finally finished with his opening, Hoar described the vessel and, using a host of diagrams and photographs and a large model of the missing *Herbert Fuller* (the barkentine had not been heard from since leaving Halifax), explained who was sleeping where in the afterhouse at the time of the crime, "Besides the captain, his wife, and the sailors, there was onboard a passenger named Lester H. Monks, a student. Like most students, he had a habit of what is called 'sporting the yoke,' which some people never get over, of locking his door at night."

Hoar also explained, "There was an ax hanging on the wall in full view of the men at meals," and then he related the sequence of events.

"Henry Slice, Falke Wassen, and Oscar Andersson had the first watch," Hoar explained, "and at twelve o'clock were relieved by Charley Brown, Frank Loheac, Hendrik Perdok, and Thomas Bram."

Hoar continued, "Bram was the guardian and protector of everybody onboard of that vessel. From his position on the deck, walking back and forth, he had an absolute view of everything that could take place onboard of that boat. Spencer the cook was fast asleep, and the three other sailors [Slice, Wassen, and Andersson] were asleep in their room. Brown was at the wheel, and Bram was walking up and down the deck. By shutting the door at the foot of the companionway, [Bram] could shut off the entryway from view."

Continuing, Hoar stated, "The second mate was the first man killed, and then the murderer walked around to the captain's cabin. He struck the captain such a hard blow that the ax stuck in [the captain's] head, and [the captain] was pulled off the bed in [Bram's] attempt to extricate the ax from the captain's head. The noise he made when he did that drew the attention of the man at the wheel."

This man was Charley Brown, who, Hoar argued, "was at one time accused of this crime," but "it was impossible for him to have left the wheel."

While referring to one of the diagrams, Hoar explained that Brown had been "holding the wheel with one hand," when he "leaned over and looked into that window and saw the murderer strike his victim another blow, with what he could not exactly say, but it looked exactly like the handle of an ax. He saw the murderer wield the weapon."

Terrified by what he had just seen, Brown "drew back with fear and trembling. Then he saw the mate disappear in the direction of that door and immediately heard a most fiendish woman's shriek. We shall prove that that shriek awoke Lester Monks."

Hoar said that, in contrast to Monks, Bram claimed not to have heard the shriek but should have, if he had merely been an "innocent man walking the deck at the time of the murders."

Hardly innocent, however, later that morning Bram had cleverly pointed out the ax on deck before Monks or Spencer could see it and then insisted it should be thrown overboard. Spencer protested but Monks, Hoar explained, still believed Bram's story about a mutiny and had agreed. Bram's trick worked.

Then, Hoar continued, "Bram said, 'We must not blame the living for the dead. This is my idea of how it occurred. The captain went to his wife's room and found the second mate assaulting her. The captain killed his wife with the ax, then attacked the second mate, who took the ax from him and killed the captain, then took the ax on deck and went back to his berth and died.'" (The absurdity of this scenario brought forth laughter in the courtroom.)

Hoar went on, "That was Bram's theory of the murders, and so powerful was his authority onboard at that time that every man signed it at his direction."

Hoar then told the jury that initially "Brown was arrested with Bram for the murders, [but] I claim that he had nothing to do with the murders."

In fact, Hoar pointed out that, when helping intern the victims in the jolly boat, "Brown cared for the bodies tenderly, handled every one of them, and suggested how they be placed in the boat," showing that "there are some incidents which come out of men's hearts which make us sure of the kind of men that do them. This is what protects virtue, though suspicion may be cast at a man."

Hoar then sought to address two incidents that might cast suspicion on Brown. The first was that "Brown had worn overalls when putting the bodies in the boat, and some of the blood had got through the overalls." Fearing that he could be arrested based on having this blood on his clothes, Hoar explained that Brown had naturally wanted to wash it off.

The second was that a "day or two before he had told a yarn of how, some years before, when in Rotterdam, he had some money and a sweetheart, and someone wanted to take both from him, and he shot the man. Then he undertook to keep the police off, went and locked himself in, and drank some beer, and escaped on the plea of insanity."

Hoar promised the jurors, however, that "when you see Brown, you will judge how probable that statement was."

Although confident that Brown would make an excellent witness, Hoar would still need the supporting testimony of others, and so he readied the jurors for a shock.

"Spencer," he stated, "is a colored man."

Apologetically, Hoar explained, "The Lord—unfortunately—does not give it into my hands to make the kind of witnesses we would like to produce to you here, but you will judge them as they appear."

After Hoar had concluded his introduction, no less than ten witnesses were called to verify such facts as the ownership of the barkentine and the names of those who signed aboard the vessel on July 1. Some of those testifying had been called from Halifax, including Ingraham, the US consul, and when it was his turn to testify, the hearing he had conducted in July came under scrutiny.

On cross-examination, Cotter got Ingraham to confirm that the hearing had been closed to the public but that Lester Monks and his father and uncle, plus his private attorney Forbes, were present during the entire proceedings.

"Why was this permitted?"

"I thought those with a direct interest in the case should be allowed to attend," Ingraham answered.

Why, Cotter wanted to know, had Forbes been allowed to cross-examine the mate because "you knew that the position of Mr. Monks and Mr. Bram at that time was somewhat antagonistic."

Ingraham insisted that anything Bram told Forbes had been voluntary, but Cotter countered that Bram was told he was free not to answer the lawyer's questions, and therefore Bram's statements at the hearing should be excluded as evidence.

After considering Cotter's argument, the two judges ruled that, for now, Bram's testimony in Halifax would not be presented to the jury.

An engineer named William A. Macdonald, hired by Hoar to survey the *Herbert Fuller* when it was still in Halifax, then provided expert testimony so poorly prepared that it tested the judges' and Cotter's patience.

Despite frantically reworking his calculations and admitting that he now "forgot" some of his measurements and had failed to make others, Macdonald stated he was certain that the window through which Brown claimed to have seen Bram kill Captain Nash was eleven inches wide and fourteen inches long. He also said that the window had two glass panes protected by seven iron bars on the outside with one and two-thirds inches of space between each bar.

Macdonald was also sure that, from inside the chart room, the window could be closed to the outside world by a curtain hanging by hooks from a rod. The distance on the afterdeck from the spoke of the wheel to the middle of the window, Macdonald stated, measured four feet.

In terms of the wheel itself, Cotter asked, "Was there anything on the wheel to fasten it?"

"Yes, sir. There was a rope with a loop on either side to fasten it."

"What kind of rope?"

"Manila, an inch in diameter, and long enough to reach from the shaft of the wheel to the spoke."

"What was the rope for?"

Here, Hoar objected, but the question was allowed.

"As I understand it, to lash the wheel," Macdonald answered.

Dr. Finn had also been called from Halifax, and as one Nash brother and two Nash aunts listened from the spectators' benches, the coroner used dolls and a grinning white skull to describe, in pitiless detail, the savage blows that had rained down on their hapless relatives. Under questioning, Finn said that, because of the long delay between death and autopsy, it had been impossible to determine if "criminal assault" had been attempted on Laura Nash.

When it was Monks's turn to testify, Judge Webb ordered the police to go out and quiet a noisy mob in the corridor that was pressing to get inside.

Still months shy of his twenty-first birthday, Monks was dressed in a suit of brown tweed, wore a high white collar with a McKinley plaid tie, and sported a mustache. He looked nervous as he took long and uncertain strides toward the stand, but in the friendly hands of Hoar, he grew visibly more confident and relaxed.

No new information emerged as Hoar gently guided his witness through the events of July 3 to 21, with Monks strictly adhering to the story prepared for him by attorneys Forbes and Hemenway. When Hoar had finished with his questioning, Cotter stepped up to cross-examine. He was not so kind.

"Now, haven't you stated you were to take this sea voyage for the benefit of your health?" asked Cotter after determining that the voyage idea had come from Dr. Monks, the witness's uncle.

"Yes, sir."

"Had you been ill?"

"Well, I don't know exactly what you would call it. I had a series of colds through the winter for the last two years, colds and a sore throat, and he thought it would be better for me to take a trip to some warm climate and be away from the New England winter for at least one year."

"New England winter?"

"Yes, sir."

"So, you decided to take it in July?"

"I should not have been home, if everything had gone well at that time, until the next June anyway."

"How long had you been suffering from illnesses?"

"For about two years."

"Was that the only trouble you were suffering from, the throat?"

"Yes, sir."

"Did you have medicine with you?"

"I had a little medicine chest, which I have now, a common thing, to use with medicines, such as headache powder and pills. That is all."

"Did you apply medicine to any part of your body?"

Here the district attorney objected, and so Cotter rephrased the question, "Didn't you state you were under treatment for certain parts?"

"No, sir."

"Now, in your room was your attention at any time called to any cloth that appeared to be covered with blood? Did you make an explanation of that, what it was used for?"

"Nobody ever called my attention to such a thing."

"Didn't you onboard the vessel state that you were suffering from a disease of a private character?"

"Never."

Under continued questioning by Cotter, Monks presented as being uniquely uninformed about certain things. Asked Cotter, "Who had charge of your room?"

"I don't know."

"Who made your bed?"

"I don't know whether it was Mrs. Nash or Spencer."

"You never knew who made your room up between the third to the thirteenth of July?"

"I never did."

Monks also said he didn't know if the door between his and the captain's wife's cabin was locked and had been unaware that the captain's revolver was between his two mattresses until found six days after the murders.

"How thick was the mattress?" Cotter wondered.

"Three inches."

"And you didn't know it was there?"

"No."

Cotter had a host of other questions for Monks, as well. Among them: Had he specifically requested the room next to the captain's wife? Why did he keep a revolver under his pillow? Why did he not see Mrs. Nash when he looked into her room? Why didn't he ask Bram why he threw the board at him? Why did he not check on Captain Nash, lying prone on the carpet, when he returned to change out of his pajamas? Why did his initial accounts of the tragedy so closely resemble the Clark Russell story he had read just hours earlier?

Monks kept his composure and had perfectly innocent explanations for everything, but seemed stymied when attempting to explain his authorship of the paper he wrote and signed, twice, on July 14.

Asked Cotter, "Were you the one who suggested that the second mate was committing an indecent assault on the captain's wife?"

"No, Mr. Bram suggested it."

"You never said a word about it."

"No."

"Never thought of it?"

"No."

"You felt at liberty to do as you pleased onboard the vessel, being a passenger and having paid your fare?"

"Within the boundaries of reason, yes."

"You did not take orders or directions from the mate before that night?"

"No."

"Was not every word in that paper written by you?"

"Yes, to the best of my knowledge."

"Written freely?"

"Yes."

"Your composition?"

"Then why do you call it Bram's version of the tragedy?"

"Because he suggested it."

"That is the only reason you had for writing it?"

"I don't see why I should not write it when he said, 'You can write best.'"

Cotter then stated, "It has been suggested here that you attended Harvard University."

"Yes," confirmed Monks.

"For how long a time?"

"In my second year."

Cotter confronted Monks with the various misspellings in the paper, and Monks acknowledged they were all his with the exception of *Cayane*, which he said had been given to him by Bram.

Returning to the contents of the paper, Cotter asked, "Why did you write it?"

"Because I was told to. It was suggested to me at the time, and I adopted it. Some things were told me, and some I wrote from my own observation."

"Did Bram say he was a 'heavy sleeper' and the 'murder might have been committed before I woke up'?"

"That was mine."

Having gone as far as he could with this line of questioning, Cotter asked Monks about his earlier reasons for suspecting Bram, "Didn't you say something about spots of blood on his suspenders?"

"No, sir."

"Not to anybody?"

"No, sir."

"Did you [say this] before Commissioner Fiske?"

"I don't remember."

"Did you see spots on the suspenders?"

"No, sir, I did not."

Continuing, Cotter asked, "Had it been represented to you that the mate said you knew more about this case than you told?"

"No, sir. Nobody ever said that to me."

"Were you not afraid, Mr. Monks, that you would be charged with this tragedy, with having something to do with it?"

"Never entered my head."

Here Cotter asked, Why then in Halifax had "you [been] acting under advice of counsel?"

"My father did that," responded Monks, explaining that he personally didn't think it necessary.

"However, that counsel came with you to Boston?"

"At my father's wish, yes, sir."

Referring to Brown's arrest onboard the barkentine, Cotter asked, "Did you ever state that any mistake was made in regard to ironing Brown?"

"No, sir."

"And you knew that he was held as a prisoner up here [in Boston] at the time of the preliminary hearing last July?"

"Yes, sir."

"And you never stated that a mistake was made in having him ironed, did you?"

"Not that I know of, no sir."

It was almost five when Monks was finally released from the stand and undoubtedly the twelve men of the jury looked forward to the trial day being over. The two judges, however, did not want to waste a minute, and since there were a few minutes left, instructed Hoar to call his next witness.

The witness duly took the stand, and after being administered the oath, Hoar asked, "Mr. Brown, what is your real name?"

"Justus Leopold Westerberg."

The witness had barely time to explain that he had first been called *Charley Brown* in Quebec because *Justus Leopold Westerberg* was too hard to pronounce, when court was adjourned for the day.

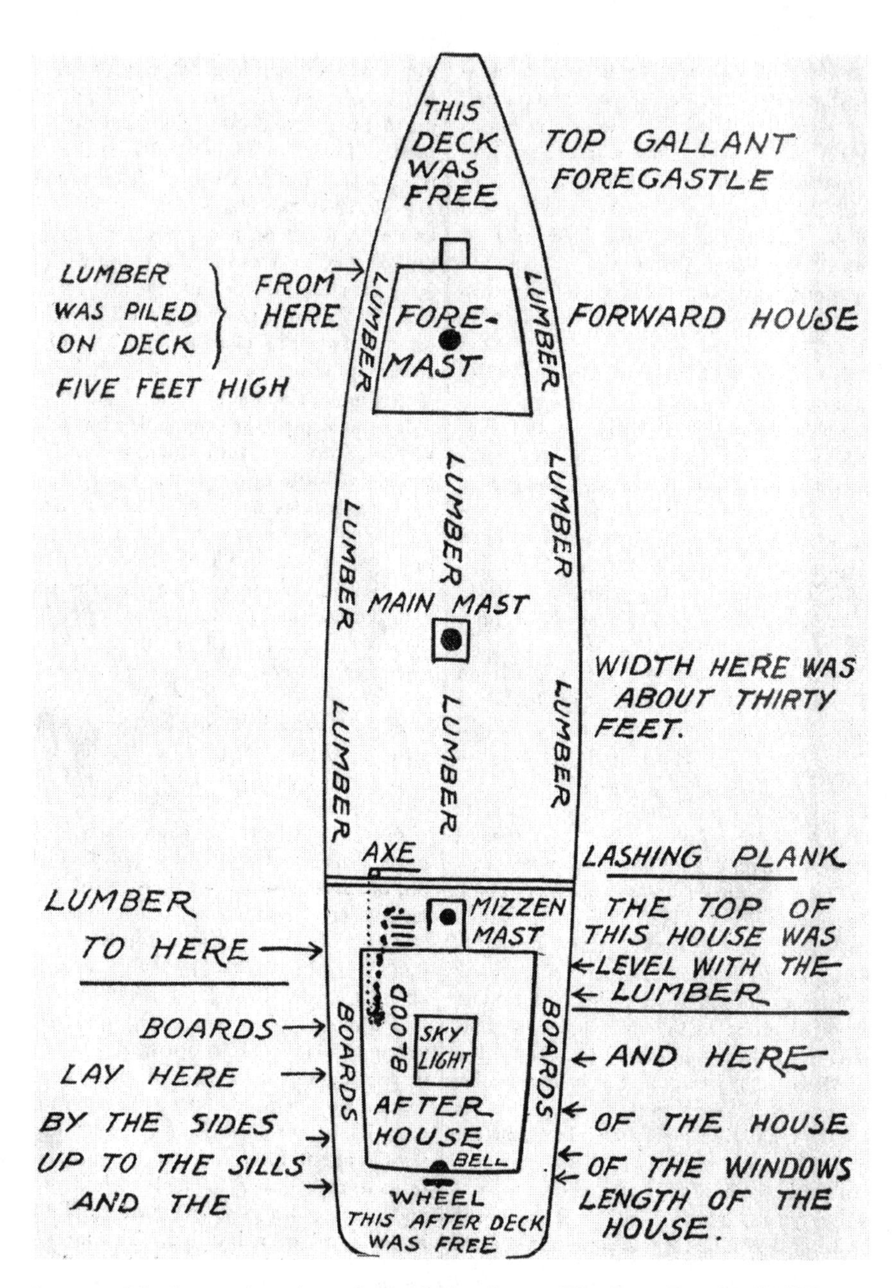

Layout of the forward, main, and afterdecks. ***Source: The Green Bag*****, April 1897.**

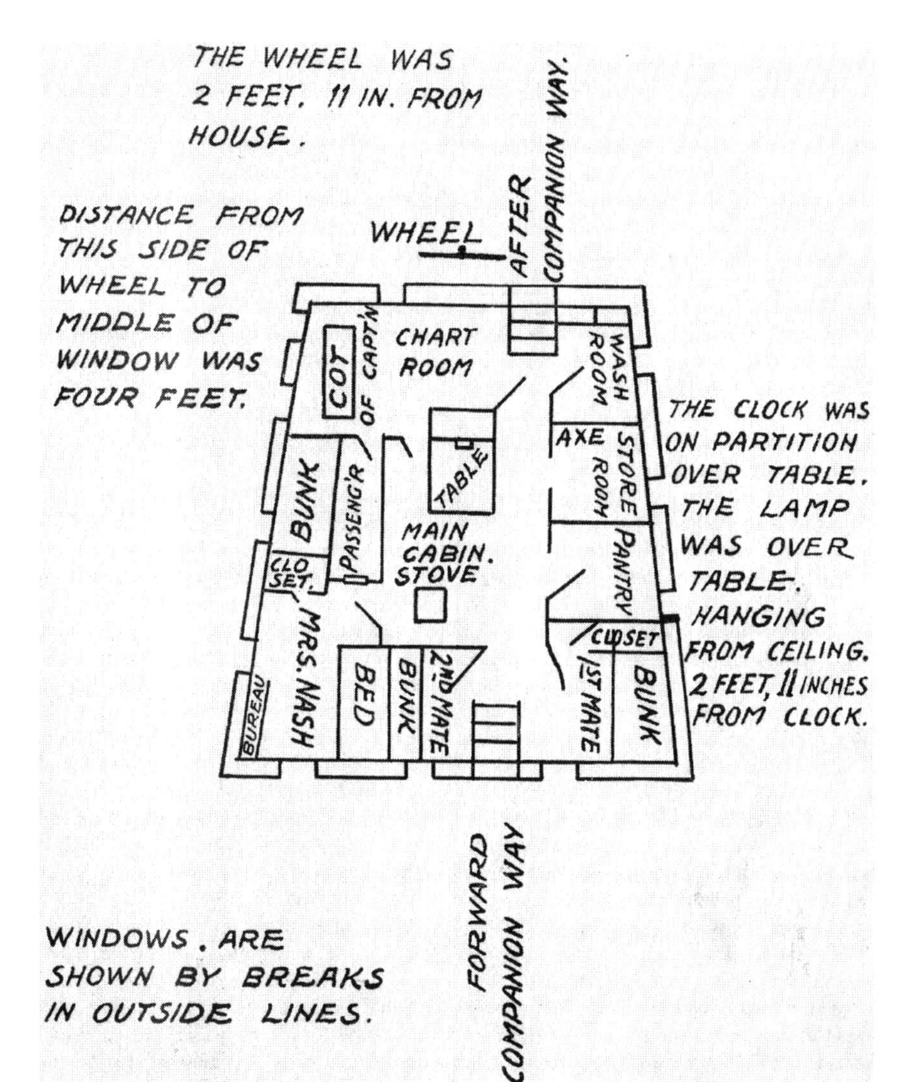

Layout of the afterhouse. ***Source: The Green Bag*****, April 1897.**

The *Herbert Fuller* anchored in Halifax Harbor, July 21, 1896. The following nine photographs were taken that same day. *Source:* Museum of Nova Scotia.

In the afterhouse, looking through the forward companionway. The main deck and the deck load of white pine boards stacked five feet high can be seen at the top of the stairs. *Source:* Museum of Nova Scotia.

In the main cabin, looking aft. The dining table is center; above it is the swinging lantern and, on the partition next to the table, the clock. On the left is the passageway to the chart room. A portion of the aft chart-room wall can be seen and, above at left, a corner of the main cabin skylight. To the right of the table is another passageway to the chart room, through which can be seen the steps of the aft companionway leading to the aft deck and wheel. *Source:* Museum of Nova Scotia.

In the chart room looking forward. On the right is the chest "a," in front of which the captain slept on a cot and mattress. In the center is the stateroom "B," where the passenger slept, and beyond that is the stateroom "C," where the captain's wife slept. To the left is a partial view of the main cabin "D," showing the coal stove and a corner of the dining table. *Source:* Museum of Nova Scotia.

Looking into the passenger's stateroom and bunk "a" and the adjoining stateroom the bed "B" belonging to the captain's wife. In this view the doorway between the two rooms is open. *Source:* Museum of Nova Scotia.

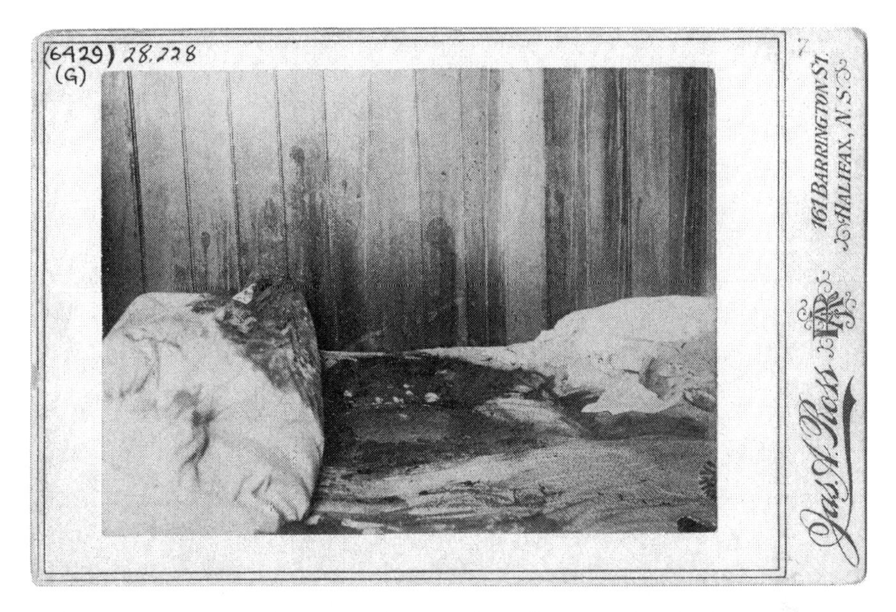

Inside the stateroom belonging to the captain's wife. Note the blood on her mattress, sheets, pillows, and wall. *Source:* Museum of Nova Scotia.

Another view of the gore. *Source:* Museum of Nova Scotia.

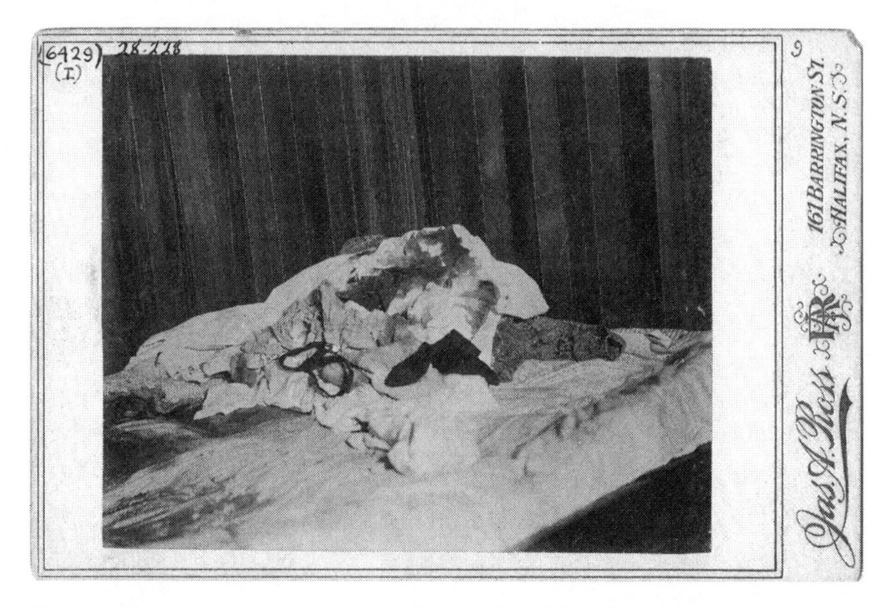

Her bloodied garters, stockings, and other clothing heaped in a pile. *Source:* Museum of Nova Scotia.

Inside the second mate's stateroom. This is his bunk and blood-stained mattress. *Source:* Museum of Nova Scotia.

On the aft deck, looking forward. Here can be seen the wheel, aft wall of the afterhouse, ladder to the afterhouse roof, and the small barred window to the chart room. (Note that, in this photograph, taken while the *Herbert Fuller* was at anchor, the wheel is held in place by a rope. Securing the wheel in this manner was called "lashing" the wheel or placing it "in beckets.") *Source:* Museum of Nova Scotia.

The six sailor-witnesses and their two keepers pose for a photograph. From left to right, standing: Bailiff Ruhl, Falke Wassen, Oscar Andersson, Deputy Marshal McGonagal. From left to right, sitting: Henry Slice, Hendrik Perdok, Charley Brown, Frank Loheac. *Source:* Boston Anthenæum.

Charley Brown. *Source:* Boston Anthenæum.

The *Herbert Fuller* in East Boston, April 1898, where it was visited by the jury.
Source: Historic New England.

Height	1 m 70.2	Head lgth	18.5	L Foot	26.0	Color L Eye	Class 5	Age 42
Eng Hgt	5 — 7	Head wdth	14.5+	L Mid F	11.7		Areola Clmar	Apparent age
Out A	1 m 76.2	Cheek wdth	14.0–	L Lit F	9.2+		Periph	Nativity St. Kitts Island (British)
Trunk	91.1	R Ear lgth	6.1 pro 2	L Cubit	48.1		Pecul	Occupation Sea Captain

Remarks relative to Measurements

1516

Forehead		Nose				R Ear		
	Inc V		Profile	Bridge r (hump)			Sup Bor g i	Hair d ch gra Beard id
	Hght 7			Base (el) Root sha			Pos Bor g op	Complexion sallow
	Width m		DIMENSIONS				Lobe fro	
	Pecul		Height g	Projection g	Breadth m		Teeth None	Weight 160
			Pecul				Chin high vert	Build m

Examined Dec 5, 1906 145-6=189

By J M Nye

Thomas Bram not long after his transfer to the US penitentiary in Atlanta. *Source:* National Archives at Atlanta.

The *Alvena* in Australia, date unknown, during its Pacific career. *Source:* Brodie Collection, La Trobe Picture Collection, State Library of Victoria.

CHAPTER 7

Brown stood again at the witness stand the following morning. Charles E. Grinnell, a Boston lawyer with no connection to the trial but attending out of curiosity, described the witness as being "of short stature, with fair hair and a great moustache, from behind which sounded a voice trained to do service in storms. A large, muscular neck held his head up straight and tossed it back now and then as he talked."

Resuming his testimony for Hoar from yesterday, Brown recalled that, before joining the *Herbert Fuller*, he had never seen Captain Nash but had met the defendant, Bram, while at the shipping office when he signed his papers. Once aboard the vessel, Brown said he was placed on Bram's watch, the port watch.

When asked if he had witnessed any interactions between Bram and Blomberg, Brown stated that one time, when the barkentine was still at Nantasket Roads, "I heard the chief mate say to the second mate, 'I want you to do what I tell you—don't intend to run me.' So the second mate answered back again, 'I don't want you to run me either.'"

"Did you ever hear any other conversation between them?" asked Hoar.

"Never, sir."

"On the night of the killing, what time did you go on watch?"

"At twelve o'clock."

Brown testified that he had gone to bed at eight thirty that evening, knowing that at midnight he and Loheac and Perdok would be called to duty on Bram's watch. Shortly before midnight, Brown explained to

Hoar, Andersson summoned him aft, and then at midnight, he took his place at the wheel behind the binnacle on the stern deck. His trick at the wheel, Brown said, was to last until the middle of the watch, two o'clock, after which time Loheac would relieve him so he could have an hour's rest in the forecastle before having to relieve Perdok at lookout at three o'clock. Then at four the starboard watch, led by the second mate, would work the ship until eight o'clock, at which time the port watch would take over again.

Brown testified that, when he assumed the wheel at midnight, it was dark and cloudy, with a fair wind coming from the quarter. The barkentine, he said, was running with all its sails—fore headsail, mainsail, main gaff topsail, spanker, and mizzen gaff topsail—set. He said that he could see the second mate, Blomberg, walking the deck on the starboard side in front of the afterhouse but after a few minutes lost sight of him. Brown said he also saw Bram walking the deck and continued to see him there, on and off, for the next hour or so, until Bram appeared in an entirely different place.

"Now just as slowly as you can and as distinctly," urged Hoar, "tell us what called your attention to him, and do it slowly now, Brown. Go ahead."

Referring to the little window to the right of the wheel where he stood steering, Brown said, "I looked through the window. I heard some noise. I was scared and took a jump to myself."

"What did you do?"

"I looked through the window on the starboard side, about four feet away from me; I saw the bed was upset."

"What bed?"

"The bed the captain was sleeping in. I saw the man lying down on the floor. I could see about half his body, from his feet up."

"Then what did you do?"

"I looked at my compass again."

"Why did you look back at your compass?"

"To see if my vessel was on course."

After checking his compass, Brown said, he again looked through the window to the chart room and noticed that someone in addition to the captain was down there.

"Who was that?"

"The mate Bram, sir."

"What did he have on?"

"Dark suit of clothes. I don't know what else. A common straw hat with a small hole in the upper part of it."

"Had you ever seen that hat before?"

"Yes, sir, every day, sir."

"On whom?"

"The mate Bram's head, sir."

"Did you see anything then?"

"I saw him lift a weapon—I could not say what kind of a weapon it was; I saw the handle. It looked to be on an ax; it was a long handle. I saw a blow fall in the same direction of the captain's head."

"You saw a blow fall? Did you see how Bram held that weapon?"

"No, sir, only saw the blow fall."

"Do you know whether he held it in one hand?"

"Only in his right hand, sir."

To illustrate, Brown then mimicked a series of quick chops with his own right hand.

"Then did you see him do anything more?"

"No, sir. He walked right out, so I be awfully scared and nervous."

"What next took place?"

"I heard a scream from Mrs. Nash, high enough so I can hear. Next I saw mate Bram on deck a little time after that."

"You had to keep moving the helm all the time?"

"To keep the vessel on her course. It was a fair wind."

"Did you ever see the wheel ropes used on that vessel when she was sailing with a fair wind?" asked Hoar, referring the practice of putting the wheel in beckets.

"Never, sir."

Returning to Bram's actions once he reappeared on deck, and using a pencil and a diagram provided by Hoar, Brown testified, "He passed by me, between me and the binnacle. I watched him sharp to see if he carried a weapon, watched for a chance to jump overboard. I was scared that he would kill me. He passed by this companionway. He just bent his head down like this and looked through, he didn't stop. The same time he passed by me, I smelled liquor from him, and he came right back again the same road he came from."

"Then where did you see him next?"

"I see him there," Brown answered, pointing the pencil to a spot near the mizzen rigging. "From that time, the time he came from aft, I didn't see where he went that time. He went for a few minutes, and then I see him come from the port side over to here, sir. He be staying there, walked from one side to the other. He reports to Frank and says, 'Four bells.' Frank was to relieve me at two o'clock."

"Then what happened?"

"Frank came out and relieved me from the wheel. I went down in the forecastle and put a blue flannel shirt outside of my cotton shirt and put a pair of heavy gray wool pants, put them outside my thin pants, and I went on, and then I light my pipe. At three o'clock I have to relieve Hendrik. I have to take charge of the lookout then."

Brown recalled that Hendrik Perdok kept him company while he stood lookout on the starboard side of the forward house. He said he was also aware of two men on deck behind him, sitting by the rail amidships, but in the dark failed to recognize them as being Bram and Monks. Then at daybreak, Brown explained, "The steward came forward, carrying a revolver in his hand. So, he asked us, 'What time did you see the second mate last?' So, I told him the last time I see the second mate was twelve o'clock, that time I went to the wheel, walking back and forth on the starboard side, fore and aft."

In his halting English, Brown related the rest of his story up until the "burial" in the jolly boat, at which he helped make the boat's canvas lining and cover.

"I asked mate Bram for a palm and needle and twine," Brown explained. "He said, 'There is a palm down in the second mate's room'—small, little bag used to carry for the palm and needle and wax and such things. So, I went down myself. I opened the door of the second mate's room, and on the left-hand side as I went in, I looked around and saw the bag. I took the bag in my left hand and walked out, shut the door after me."

At this, Hoar prompted, "And when you walked out, you didn't know then that there was any blood on the bottom of the bag?"

"No, sir. So, I walked up and twist my left leg against the bottom of the bag, and as soon as I got up on deck, I see there were two spots, black, looked like pieces of liver."

"Where?"

"On my left leg, sir—on my white pair of pants."

Realizing that his overalls had blood on them, Brown said that he then changed into a new pair. Hoar asked what Brown did with the pair that had blood on them.

"Threw them overboard."

"When was that?"

"Tuesday afternoon."

"Who was present when you threw them overboard?" asked Hoar.

"I don't recollect—a good many people, two or three of my shipmates. It was down near the forecastle. It was after everything were done."

"What was on those overalls?"

"There was lots of blood and other kinds of dirt. Of course, we had lots of dirty work the day the people were killed."

Again being led by Hoar, Brown testified that he was put in irons at about five o'clock the next morning, Wednesday, July 15. Brown explained that, having barely slept for the past forty-eight hours and trying to get some sleep, "I was covered up in my oilskin coat, all over my head and body, too."

Then, Brown explained, "All I heard was the steward, Spencer, swearing and cursing over me, calling me all the names he can find out, bad names. He says, 'You do wrong.' The steward says, 'You have killed those people, and you have been down in the cabin and stealing the captain's revolver.'"

Brown stated that he was put in irons and placed in the well around the mizzenmast.

"Now, up to the time you were put in irons, had you said—had you any conversation with anybody about the killing?" asked Hoar.

"No, sir, [but] Mr. Bram came aft, and he came forward here, sir, on the starboard side. He stopped here and said, 'Look at me,' he says. 'You thought,' he said to me, 'you should be smart. You thought you should be smart and put me in irons. And I am too clever for you,' he says."

Hoar, bringing his witness back to the hour of the murders, produced a photograph taken in Halifax from the stern deck of the *Herbert Fuller*.

"Is that a correct representation of the part of the wheel, the afterhouse, and the ladder and the little window as it was on the morning of July 14?"

"I remember everything; that is right, sir. The place that the ladder stands is the right place. Everything like that is correct. That ladder stood close to that hatch."

"Between the time you went on watch at midnight on the night of the thirteenth and fourteenth of July until you were relieved by Frank Loheac, did you leave the wheel?"

"Never, sir."

"Did you take your hand from it?"

"Never, sir."

"When you looked through that window, how did you hold the wheel?"

"I held it—there is a spindle through the arm, and the men always are supposed to stand that way to the spindle."

"Now, when you were looking through the window, what were you holding onto?"

"To the spokes of that wheel."

"With how many hands?"

"Both hands. I must move the wheel all the time for keeping the vessel on her course with the breeze we had that night."

The district attorney concluded his direct examination not long before Judge Colt and Judge Webb called a midday break for dinner, and when the trial resumed, the witness was in the unfriendly hands of the defense.

Cotter asked, "How long have you followed the seas?"

"Close to twenty-five years, sir."

"You never signed your name, did you, in this country other than Charles Brown?"

"Never in this country except Charles Brown. I used that name since eighty-four or eighty-five. I can show my character for that, the character I got from my ships that I got from my captains."

"Do you remember seeing a reporter down in Halifax and talking with him about your name?"

"Yes, there were so many reporters."

"Did you give him a reason for changing your name?"

"I don't recollect that. I see that paper afterward."

"Did you not state to the reporter that you changed your name because you got into trouble with a captain?"

"No, sir. I never been in trouble with any captain in this world. I have a good character with any captain."

Switching the topic, Cotter asked, "As far as you could see, were all the doors open on the night of the murders?"

"Yes, sir."

Cotter then questioned Brown about the window through which he claimed to have seen Bram strike Captain Nash.

"Could the window be opened from the outside?"

"I don't know, sir."

"Did you open it?"

"No, sir."

"Did you open the curtain?"

"No, sir."

"Could you put your hands between the bars of the window?"

"I don't know, sir."

Cotter next asked Brown if, between twelve and two o'clock, he had ever taken either of his hands off the wheel.

"No, sir."

"And standing erect, Brown? Erect were you?"

"Yes, sir."

"Very well. And working the wheel?"

"Working the wheel."

"And while in that position, these here different things that you have described to this jury you saw, did you?"

"Yes, sir."

"Did you see any lantern?"

"No, sir."

"Could you see the clock from where you were?"

"No, sir."

"Could you see the man's face from where you were? The man on the lounge or bunk?"

"No, sir."

"Did you know that the captain occupied that room or slept there?"

"No, sir."

"How much light was there in that room?"

"Well, the light was like a lamp that was turned down, but there was light enough for me to see the man inside that window."

"You knew that the lamp was in the forward, or main, cabin, didn't you?"

"I did not know where it was."

"You did not see any light where the captain was?"

"No, sir."

"At what time did you see the trouble in that room?"

"I will give the best time I can. Supposed to be half past one."

"Did you remain at the wheel about half an hour after that?"

"Yes, sir. About that, sir."

"And did you know at that time that someone had been murdered in the cabin?"

"Yes, sir."

"You did not say a word?"

"No, sir."

"You did not alarm anybody?"

"No, sir."

"You did not ring the bell?"

"No, sir."

"You knew that there were people on duty at the forward end of the ship?"

"Yes, sir."

"And by ringing the bell at the binnacle, you could have alarmed them, could you not?"

"No, sir."

"Could you have not alarmed everybody onboard the ship by ringing the bell?"

"Only ring the bell to get orders from the officers."

"Aren't you allowed to ring the bell to save the life of your captain?"

"It was too late for me to save the captain at the time I saw it."

"It has been suggested to me that you didn't know that the person struck was the captain?"

"No, sir."

"Who did you suppose occupied that room?"

"I always thought Mr. Monks, sir."

"Didn't you have an opportunity to alarm or rouse the captain to save Mr. Monks, if you thought that was Monks's room?"

"Well, I could have sung out as much as I liked."

"You could have struck the bell, couldn't you?"

"I could do anything I liked, but I saw there was a murder, and I couldn't make as much noise as I liked. I was nervous and scared. I was scared for my own life."

"And you remained at the wheel about half an hour?"

"From that time, yes, sir."

"And Frank came and relieved you at the wheel, the Frenchman?"

"Yes, sir."

"About two o'clock, half an hour later, and you didn't say a word to him about any trouble?"

"No, sir, never."

Cotter then inquired what Brown had seen through the window, and the answers Brown gave were no different than those he had supplied Hoar. Cotter also asked about Bram appearing on deck shortly after Brown had heard the screams of Mrs. Nash.

"You were not afraid of him when you saw him coming toward you after he committed the murder?"

"I was scared of him."

"But you didn't run off anywhere?"

"I had to stand there to steer the vessel."

Shifting to a new line of inquiry, Cotter gave Brown the paper on which Monks had written the theory of the murders.

"Before you wrote your name on that paper, was the paper read to you?"

"Yes, sir."

"Did you make any objection to signing it?"

"No, sir."

"Well, when you signed it, you knew the statements in that paper were not correct, didn't you?"

"I knowed it was all lie."

"Why did you sign that paper when you knew it was a lie?"

"The ship was bound to port, so I know that we have to come to the United States port and tell the truth."

"Did you say a word to anybody before you were put in irons?"

"Nothing about it. I tell my shipmates to keep quiet. Everything will be all right as soon as we come to port."

Brown added that once in irons he almost immediately told Andersson that he had witnessed the captain being killed, and that two days later, on Friday, "I tell the truth to what I see to Spencer."

Cotter then had Brown explain what he had been doing on Monday, the day before the murders, and Brown described in great length about how he had scrubbed both the afterdeck and the outside of afterhouse with sand, including around the windows. After the jurors had learned more about the scrubbing process than they probably cared to know, Cotter turned to Brown's testimony before the grand jury, testimony he gave while still being held "for probable cause" by Commissioner Fiske.

"Did you know that you would be permitted to go free," Cotter asked, "or remain in jail only as a witness if you testified before the grand jury against Bram?"

"I understand so much, if I came in before the grand jury, and the grand jury saw me, and they did not find any bill against me, I would be set free."

"Who told you that? Did anyone tell you by coming before the grand jury they would find no bill?"

"I didn't know anything about that when I came in."

"Before Mr. Waters, the deputy marshal, came for you, didn't you know you were going to be called before the grand jury to testify against Bram?"

"No, sir."

Cotter again changed the subject, "Mr. Brown, have you ever been in an insane asylum?"

"I beg pardon. I don't understand that."

"Were you ever in a crazy house?"

"No, sir."

"Do you remember having a talk with Frank Loheac?"

"Yes, sir."

"Did you tell him that you were?"

"I don't remember what I told him. I remember little, sir."

"You remember a little something?"

"Yes, sir."

"Don't you remember you told him that you were in one in Rotterdam?"

"No, sir."

When pressed further by Cotter, the witness protested, "We were spinning yarns, sir."

"Well, you did tell him that you shot a man in Rotterdam?"

"I did, sir."

"Did you say to him you got out of it on the plea of insanity?"

"That is more than I recollect to say."

"You don't remember about that?"

"No, sir. I don't remember everything I say. I used to spin lots of yarns."

"Were you in Rotterdam in July 1891?"

"I don't know, sir, what time I was in Rotterdam. I don't know, sir. I don't recollect what time it was."

"Did you not say to Frank Loheac that you used a horse pistol, and you shot a man, that you shot him dead, then you locked your doors, you finished drinking a bottle of beer and smoking your pipe before you let the police in?"

"No, sir."

"You did not say that?"

"No, sir. I say, I told him I shot a man. I remember I say that. I lose my money and my girl."

"And your girl?"

"Yes. And then I have to go to sea again."

"Did you tell him how you escaped from that trouble?"

"No, sir."

"Well, was that story true?"

"Yes."

Here Judge Webb interjected, saying, "That is not quite it," so Cotter rephrased the question, "Is it true that you shot him?"

"No, sir. It is a lie. That is only a story."

"Did you ever know a man named Peter Van Bommel?"

"No, sir. No, sir."

"When were you last in Rotterdam?"

Brown said it was 1890 or 1891, when he signed aboard a ship that ran between that city and New York.

Cotter then asked, "Now, give attention to this question. On the twelfth of July 1891, did you shoot at one Peter Van Bommel?"

"No, sir. I don't know the man. I don't know the name, sir."

"In Rotterdam?"

"I know Rotterdam."

"And were you not confined to the insane asylum?"

"No, sir."

"Afterward?"

"No, sir"

"Do you now say, Mr. Witness, that the whole story you told Frank at the forecastle in regard to shooting a man is false?"

"I might say it, and I might not. I tell lots of yarns."

"Was that story which you told Frank at the forecastle about shooting a man at Rotterdam, was that true or not?"

"That is true I told him. I says—"

"You told him, but did you shoot the man?"

"No, sir. I never shoot the man, never, in the name of God."

"So, what you said to Frank was not true?"

"It was only a yarn, a story."

"It did not have a word of truth in it, did it?"

"No, sir. I never shot a man in no part of the world. Never shot at no man. Never killed a man, either."

After the pressure placed on him by Cotter, Brown must have felt relieved when Hoar asked some easy questions on a redirect examination, but then it was Cotter's turn again. Cotter arose from his chair slowly, walked to the witness stand, and asked, "You read English, Mr. Brown?"

"A very little, sir."

"Would you be good enough to read that?"

Here Cotter handed the witness some pieces of paper.

"I don't think it."

"Will you try?"

"I no can read it."

"You cannot?"

"No, sir. I don't understand. I don't understand some words."

"You do not know what it is about, do you?"

"No, sir."

"Can you read print?"

"A little, sir. A little."

Suddenly Hoar shouted, "What does this purport to be? Brown, put that down!"

The witness dropped the papers, and all at once the lawyers began arguing with each other. The two judges, calling for order, told Brown to step off the stand. Then Cotter's junior counsel, French, picked the papers off the floor and, approaching the bench, declared calmly and slowly, with every word distinct, "If your honors please, there are certain matters which are connected with these papers to be called to the attention of the court, which we should like the privilege of discussing with the court, without the presence of the jury."

The jury, along with Brown, was excused, and addressing the justices once again, French said, "We desire to ask a postponement in order to prove things, which we believe upon our counsel of this court, that we can prove beyond a reasonable doubt, to show that the man who has just left the stand has committed perjury, and your honors will understand that upon the testimony of that man the life of our client might depend, and the circumstances under which we ask this grace of the court, not for ourselves, but for our client, are these.

"At about the time this defendant was arraigned, not long before, we received information in a casual way with reference to a certain offense committed by the witness who has just left the stand, in Rotterdam, and his commitment to an insane asylum. Your honors will remember that, at the time of the arraignment and when we were discussing the date of the trial, we alluded to that fact and asked leave for sufficient time to prove those facts, whereupon the district attorney [Hoar] arose and said, before the court and to us in the most positive and solemn manner, that he had made thorough inquiries and that there was utterly no foundation for the statement. We, of course, assumed at once that those inquiries had been made, as the power is given to the prosecuting officer of this government to see that there was no reasonable chance of there being any truth in this statement, but we took, nevertheless, the precaution to communicate with the American consul at Rotterdam, giving him the name, making a full statement of the facts to him as we heard them, and asking him to cable if anything of the kind had occurred and also to send the record if one there was.

"About a week ago—I have forgotten the exact date—we received a short cable from the American consul to the effect that the statement was true, with the exception that the man shot at did not die and that the record had been forwarded. This morning, while we were in court, a statement purporting to be by the chief commissioner of police in Rotterdam, who is the chief committing magistrate in that city, addressed to the United States consul in Rotterdam, was received, setting forth in detailed circumstances, which, if true, prove the man who had been upon this stand to have been guilty this morning of the crime of perjury."

In response to "Cotter's bombshell"—as the press would term the shocking development—Hoar rose and said, "This is a pretty serious matter, and I don't want to slight it, both for the defense's sake and the government's sake."

In a calm voice, Hoar assured the judges that he would personally investigate the perjury charges against his witness this evening, and although it was already four o'clock, he needed no extra time. The judges agreed to this, and, unaware of what had transpired in their absence, the jurors were called back and told they were being excused a bit early but would be back in court tomorrow morning.

The jurors duly filed out of the courtroom and as usual were escorted by their warders, who were two kindly deputies named McGonagal and Ruhl, to their quarters at the Quincy House Hotel in Scollay Square. (During these trips McGonagal and Ruhl carefully avoided Washington Street's newspaper row and all of its bold-faced bulletins screaming Bram's guilt.) Once at their temporary home, where they slept on cots in one large room, the jurors were closely monitored, being forbidden to talk about the trial or to learn anything about the world outside (one juror learned of the death of his sister only after the trial had ended).

After his first day's testimony, Brown was returned to the Charles Street Jail. There he normally would have gone to the guarded room (made as comfortable as possible under the circumstances) that he shared with the other five sailor-witnesses. Under special orders from Hoar, however, on this night Brown was locked up in a prisoner's cell as if he was the man—or could yet be the man—on trial for his life.

CHAPTER 8

Brown was roused early in the morning and taken from his cell to the federal building and then to the district attorney's office. He and Hoar had a talk. When the jury was seated and court readjourned, Brown was once again on the stand.

Prompted Hoar, "In answer to certain questions by Mr. Cotter, you stated that you had not shot a man in Rotterdam or shot at one or been in an insane asylum there. I should like to have you tell of any transaction that took place there relating at all to any such transaction as I have described. Go on."

"I came from Antwerp and left a Nova Scotia ship."

"Came from Antwerp and left a Nova Scotia ship?"

"The ship *Honolulu*, Captain Daniel Leary. Last port we came was Tacoma, Washington."

"Now, state what you did from there on."

"I was paid off, thirty sovereigns. I want to go home and see my sisters and brothers I hadn't seen for years."

"Where did they live?"

"Copenhagen. I took the train from Antwerp to Rotterdam for to take the steamboat there, and on the passage to Antwerp, I feel sick. I commenced getting scared about everybody I see around me in the railroad. I thought they were going to do me some harm, steal my money."

"Yes, go on."

Brown recounted how he was looking for a man named Stamm, with whom he had stayed before, in the city.

"The time I came to Rotterdam, I met a man at the station. I asked this man, Does he know Stamm? And he says, 'Yes, sir.' So, that man went along with me down the street. I met Stamm on the street. I had been boarding with him a couple of nights when I was at Rotterdam before from ships, ashore from liberty. So, I asked him if he couldn't give me room for the night.

"He says, 'No, my wife is dead, and I am broke down, Charley.' He would take me to a place where I could get a room. Took me to a Scandinavian. His name was Edward—that is all I know—his name is Edward."

"Did you stay there?"

"I stayed there, sir. Came about four o'clock that afternoon. So, I feel sick and want to go to bed. I took two dollars from my pocket and gave them to Stamm. I undressed me, I get my clothes up in my room, where the bed is, where I sleep. I went to my bed, and lying there about an hour or two, the man I boarded with, Edward, he came home. So, he talked with me, and I told him I would like to have this room for my own part. I don't like to see a stranger come in.

"He said, 'It is all right Charley.' So, we were sitting and talking for an hour or so. I went to bed, and I lie awake for about four or five hours. I couldn't go to sleep."

"Laid awake for four or five hours?"

"Yes, I couldn't go to sleep. So, from that time I left the home and until about eleven days from there, I don't know anything about myself."

"And when did you first know about yourself?"

"About fourteen days later in a hospital. There was a doctor, sir, a physician. He asked me if I knew where I was. I says, 'No.' So, he told me, 'You are in a hospital.' I says, 'What are you doing here, sir?' He says, 'Don't be afraid. Be glad, for what has happened is all forgiven.'

"He says, 'You have lost your senses. Do you know what you have been doing?' I says, 'No, sir.'

"He says, 'That place you were boarding, there was somebody come into your room, and you fired off a revolver.'"

Hoar, as if he just heard this story for the first time, asked, "You fired off a revolver?"

"He told me, sir, and that shot entered a window. He says, 'Don't be frightened or nervous, for everything was forgiven.'"

Brown then launched into a detailed account of how thirty sovereigns had gone missing from his trunk during his stay in the hospital, but Cotter objected to the digression, and Hoar, concurring, told Brown, "That is all," and turned his witness over to the defense.

Cotter, visibly irate, demanded of Brown, "Didn't you remember yesterday when you were on the stand that you were in an insane asylum with crazy people?"

"I know I was at a hospital, sir."

"Well, weren't you asked if you were not in a hospital?"

"Yes, I am not sure myself whether I do shoot one. I know three people tell me."

"Didn't you understand that I was asking you about that same subject yesterday, whether you were in the hospital and whether you had shot at a man?"

"Yes, sir."

"Why didn't you answer me as you did Mr. Hoar?"

"I don't know what I had done more than three people tell me."

"Well, you knew then as well as you did when you talked with Mr. Hoar out in his office, didn't you?"

"Just the same, sir."

Pointing to the jurors, Cotter asked, "Why didn't you tell these gentlemen what you told Mr. Hoar in his office yesterday?"

"Well, I won't know exactly. I know I was free of everything. I don't kill anybody. I had never been arrested."

"You knew you were in a hospital? We asked you a great many times if you were in a hospital."

Here Hoar objected, telling Cotter, "You put it in a different form," and Judge Webb agreed, saying of the witness, "He told you in the beginning that he did not know what an insane asylum was."

Cotter rephrased his question, "Don't you remember I asked you a great many times if you were in a crazy house?"

"Yes, sir, I do."

"You said you were not?"

"Yes, sir, I was not sure, and I tell it so this morning to everybody."

"And do you wish to be understood as saying now to this jury that you never knew that was an insane asylum?"

"I don't know anything about that."

No less irate than he had been at the beginning of his cross-examination, Cotter turned to the two judges and said, "That is all. Mr. French wishes to make a statement."

Brown was dismissed as a witness, and at the request of the judges, the jury was withdrawn from the courtroom.

French was now free to make his statement: "Yesterday morning, as I said in my brief argument last night, we got possession for the first time of facts which led us to believe that the important witness for the prosecution, the man upon whose testimony this charge rests or falls, was not only a perjurer, but a man suffering from homicidal mania. He was asked in the most explicit terms yesterday with reference to any affair of shooting in which he played a part in Rotterdam, his commitment in an insane asylum or crazy asylum, and his answer that there was not a word of truth in it, that it was a sea yarn. That was a statement made under oath and a statement which we have reason to believe was an absolute false statement. Will the court take the responsibility of saying, will the district attorney take the responsibility of saying, that a man's life shall depend upon the testimony of one we can show in so important respect as this—because it seems to us to be very important—was perjuring himself?"

Approaching the bench, Hoar countered, "If your honors please, the grounds are shifting so rapidly that it is a little hard for me to keep up with them in this case. Last night it was on account of the perjury of Charles Brown. This morning it is on account on a form of homicidal mania which was so severe that, if your honors will look at the testimony—not at the doctor's statement but the chief of police's statement from abroad—that he was discharged in [only] sixteen days. It seems to me that I do not have to say much more than that. The man says he was sick; the man says he went to this house. The man says he was unconscious for sixteen days. Now a man is very often unconscious in sickness; he very often has hallucinations and delirium in sickness, and there is absolutely no evidence here of any homicidal tendency whatsoever from this man. Do you suppose that skillful physicians, if this was an insane asylum, would discharge a raving maniac or a man with homicidal tendencies in [just] sixteen days or seventeen? It seems to me that that argument is puerile."

Stating that they would discuss the matter between themselves, the judges conferred alone, and ten minutes later, Webb announced their decision. It was that Cotter's request was unreasonable because it would necessitate a pause in the trial until "some indeterminate time in order that testimony may be gotten from a foreign country upon a particular matter."

The trial, the judges decreed, must go on.

Undoubtedly thrilled with his victory, which was by no means a minor one, Hoar called his next witness, Hendrik Perdok. Under questioning, the sailor said he had been born in Holland, was twenty-two years old, left school at age twelve to go sea, and had been in the United States just eleven days before signing aboard the *Herbert Fuller*. In terms of the murders, however, Perdok's testimony revealed that he knew nothing at all.

Jonathan Spencer, the "colored man" whom Hoar had earlier prepared the jury for, next took the stand.

Spencer stated, "I am twenty-four years old and was born in the British West Indies. I have been at sea for nine or ten years. I was onboard of all kinds of vessels since I first joined as cabin boy. I joined the *Herbert Fuller* last December in New York."

Questioned closely by Hoar, Spencer testified that, prior to the murders, Bram had made certain remarks to him regarding the captain and his wife. Spencer recalled, for instance, that Bram once commented of Mrs. Nash's appearance, "What a change of dress makes for a woman."

Spencer also remembered that Bram once told him that Mrs. Nash was a good wife and that Captain Nash was unworthy of her and that, if the captain died, she would marry a younger man, and Bram said, according to Spencer, "That is the way the captain's money would go."

Spencer testified that at other times Bram was critical of Mrs. Nash, dismissing her as "just a country girl" who was "putting on airs" for the college student Monks. Regarding Captain Nash, Spencer testified that Bram was often critical of him, blaming him for such things as not providing more towels. And then during the evening before the murders, Spencer testified, he saw Bram approach the captain and his wife while they were strolling on the afterhouse roof. The captain and Bram had a brief exchange of some sort that Spencer could not hear, after which Bram had turned away from the couple with an angry expression on his face. Spencer recalled that Bram then came up to him and said, "That's not natural."

Spencer left the stand at noon when, it being Saturday, court adjourned for the rest of the weekend.

The trial had already gone on for a week, and with many witnesses not yet heard from, the government and the defense were not expected to rest their respective cases until the end of the next week. This meant that in all likelihood the twelve men of the jury would spend their Christmas not at home with their families but sequestered together and deliberating Bram's fate.

Court was called to order at nine thirty Monday morning, December 21, and as usual, inside the courtroom stood four expert stenographers at their desks, set to transcribe the coming day's court proceedings into shorthand. Also sitting at their respective desks and prepared to decipher the shorthand into English were four rapid typists. An assistant helped ensure the process ran seamlessly, and not long after court would adjourn for the day, both attorneys and reporters would have copies of that day's transcript, running several hundred pages, for their review. Also inside the courtroom that morning, as usual, sat a crowd of rapt spectators, including by this time many regulars, the majority of whom, it was noted, were female.

Bram was marched in by Deputy Walters to take his seat in the prisoner's dock, and after six days of listening to testimony, most of it against him, the accused's face appeared drawn and haggard. Spencer resumed his place at the stand and testified that before the murders he witnessed Bram ordering Brown to clean some brass. Apparently offended by the order, Spencer said he heard Brown curse Bram under his breath, mumbling, "None of those God-damn bluenoses moves with me" (*bluenose* being a nickname for a Nova Scotian).

Spencer also told Hoar that Monks had once said of Bram, "He's so smart he should be in Congress."

Spencer then stated that after the murders Monks, despite his subsequent claims in the newspapers, had never once taken charge of the vessel. Spencer also revealed that the second mate, Blomberg, was a man of few words but the few he uttered were usually sarcastic, and that Blomberg had arrived on the *Herbert Fuller* while still on Long Wharf in a state of drunkenness.

Spencer said he saw Captain Nash drinking in the chart room on the afternoon before the murders. Spencer also testified that, when Bram told them they should head for French Guiana, Loheac admitted to having deserted the French navy and feared that he would be arrested by the authorities there.

While much of Spencer's testimony for Hoar was of this scattershot variety, during cross-examination Cotter got the witness to focus and in so doing severely undercut Brown's earlier testimony, although it seems Spencer wanted to get in one last dig at Captain Nash.

When questioned by Cotter on the captain's temperament, Spencer, who was the only member of the crew who had sailed previously with him, replied that he was jealous of his wife and that, on other voyages before the fateful one, he was prone to rushing into his cabin for his revolver at the slightest provocation. Spencer added that at the dining table Mrs. Nash had to get her husband's permission to talk to young Monks.

At this a juror interrupted the testimony, "How do you know that Mrs. Nash had to ask the captain for permission to speak to the passenger?"

"I have ears," replied the witness.

Then Cotter got Spencer to concentrate on the matter at hand. Could Brown, asked Cotter, have seen anything of the chart room interior from the afterdeck on the night the captain was killed? No, said Spencer, because the light from the main cabin lamp did not illuminate the chart room. Could, asked Cotter, Brown have been both at the wheel and also see inside the window? Spencer answered that he had tried this once and that it could not be done. And even if the chart room had been illuminated and even if Brown had let go of the wheel to look directly into the window, asked Cotter, could Brown have seen the captain being murdered? No, Spencer answered; on the night of the murders, the interior curtain of that window had been drawn shut. Cotter asked Spencer if he was sure of this.

"Yes, sir. It was drawn on the rod to the full length of the window, about an inch from the glass."

"How was it the next morning?"

"One end of the rod had been lifted out and was hanging down."

"Could that have been done from the outside?"

"No, sir. You could not reach the rod from the outside."

"Did you say anything about it when you noticed the rod down?"

"Yes, sir. I said, 'Who did this?' Brown said, 'I did this. I pushed the curtain aside.'"

"When did you first notice the curtain pulled aside and the rod down?"

"It was the second time, when we went down to remove the bodies, that I asked who did it, and Brown said that he did."

Spencer also spoke of something Bram had informed him: "I had a talk with Bram after Brown was put in irons, and he said he had seen Brown, while at the wheel that night, leave his place and go to the mizzen jib. I asked him why he did not stop Brown, and he said he thought Brown was merely going for something he wanted. I said, 'It was your duty to have spoken to him.'"

Spencer's overall testimony had done far more damage to the government's case than good, and Hoar must have regretted having ever called the "colored man" to the stand.

Hoar's next witness, an officer named Robert N. Lehan of Chief O'Sullivan's force, did no damage to the prosecution's case but did no good either. After Lehan attempted to testify which afterhouse doors were locked and which were unlocked on the night of the murders, Cotter objected that the Halifax policeman could not have known this based on an inspection made ten days after the fact. The judges agreed, and the officer was excused to take the next steamer home.

After this, Hoar called Falke Wassen, and the sailor testified that he was a native of Sweden, was twenty-one years old, and had followed the sea since 1893. Wassen said that, when he gave the wheel and the course to Brown at twelve o'clock, not long before the murders, the *Herbert Fuller* was running about six miles per hour and that shortly thereafter he saw Blomberg, who had earlier been sleeping on deck, standing near the forward house.

Hours after the murders, when all went into the afterhouse to see the bodies, Wassen heard Bram say, "Look at the captain. I'd die for him."

A day later, Wassen also heard Bram say, "If we don't get Brown guilty, we will get two years each."

Detective Nicholas Power was called to the stand next. Hoar asked the detective about his interview of Bram in Halifax. In particular, Hoar wanted to know what Bram had meant when, referring to Brown, Bram made the statement, "He could not see me from there."

To Power what Bram clearly meant was that, when Bram had entered the afterhouse using the forward companionway just before the murders, he thought Brown, being at the wheel and behind the afterhouse at the time, was not in the position to have witnessed this.

Cotter, however, strenuously objected to having the statement (which certainly sounded like an indirect confession) accepted as evidence. Cotter argued that Bram had been Power's prisoner at the time of the interview and that Power had taken "extraordinary liberties, such as stripping and searching him" and that "this treatment prevented the statement as being classed as a free and voluntary one."

Wanting to get to the bottom of this, in an extraordinary move, Judge Webb decided to find out for himself. From the bench, he asked Power, "You say there was no inducement to him in the way of promise or expectation of advantage?"

"Not any, your honor," the detective replied.

"Held out?"

"Not any, your honor."

"Nor anything said in the way of suggestion to him that he might suffer if he did not, that it might be worse for him?"

"No, sir. Not any."

"So far as you were concerned, it was entirely voluntary?"

"Voluntary, indeed."

After having shown how it was done, Webb handed the witness back to Cotter, who took an exception (a formal objection) to both Power being allowed to testify about the interview and to Webb, who represented the court, which was supposed to be impartial, taking over from the defense counsel and asking the witness leading questions.

Henry Slice the sailor and John Snow the undertaker were the last witnesses of the day, but neither had much to say about the murders, with Snow having so little to say that Cotter did not even bother to cross-examine him. After the jury had been escorted from the courtroom for the day (a little early because one of the jurors had a headache), Hoar rose and, without warning, landed a bombshell that he hoped might equal Cotter's of three days before.

Explaining that certain "facts" had "developed themselves in the process of the trial," Hoar declared that a man named Nicklas from

Baltimore was sitting right here in the courtroom and that, when the trial resumed tomorrow, he would like the jury to hear what this man had to say.

Explaining this request, Hoar informed the judges that Nicklas had sailed with the defendant aboard the schooner *White Wings* and that "Mr. Bram proposed to Mr. Nicklas that they should kill the captain of that vessel, take possession of her, and sail her off and dispose of her cargo."

Hoar added that this voyage was the last one taken by Bram before he signed with Captain Nash and that, like the *Herbert Fuller*, the *White Wings* had also been destined for Rosario and also carried a load of lumber.

"Mr. Nicklas laughed at the offer made by Mr. Bram," Hoar related, "and said that he would not go into it [the scheme], whereupon Bram said, 'If you don't want to kill this particular captain, let us go onboard a Norwegian vessel, where they have fewer men before the mast, where they don't talk our language, and where they are bound with coffee, which is a better cargo than lumber, and when she is going around Cape Town, we can give the crew knockout drops so that they will not know anything about it and then kill the captain, and the crew of the vessel will obey our orders.'"

Based on what Bram had also told Nicklas during the time the two were on the *White Wings*, Hoar said there had been previous instances when Bram had improperly disposed of a vessel's cargo. The first was aboard the *Twilight*, a sailing vessel captained and partly owned by Bram. According to Nicklas, after selling the cargo in port, Bram headed out to sea, where he deliberately sank the empty vessel and later told the other owners that the freight had gone down with the ship. The second, according to Nicklas, was aboard another vessel captained by Bram, the *China*, which Bram had sailed into Belize with a cargo of coconuts. Once there, Bram raised distress signals and claimed that his cargo had been damaged by water. With the help of a friend who was also an agent of a New Orleans buying house, Bram fabricated papers showing he sold the damaged cargo for just two hundred dollars. But according to Nicklas, in reality Bram had disposed of the undamaged coconuts for many times that while also profiting from the insurance claim.

Well aware that Colt and Webb might look askance at letting the jury know about Bram's past alleged piracy, the district attorney reminded the judges that in the "much-quoted Lizzie Borden case, proof that she bought prussic acid" had been allowed in as evidence because it showed a "desire on her part, or a motive, or intent to rid somebody of life." This had been permitted even though, Hoar reminded, Borden's father and stepmother "were killed with an ax" and not prussic acid.

The district attorney then bolstered his argument by citing case after case where the jury was allowed to hear evidence showing that the defendant was capable of planning and committing a crime similar to but not exactly like the one being prosecuted, and he requested that he be allowed to do so, too.

The moment the district attorney concluded his request, Cotter jumped up from his seat and shouted, "This is the most extraordinary position ever taken by the government at the trial of a capital or any other case. It is done, I daresay, for newspaper effect because the government realizes its case is weak, and this effort was made for the purpose of prejudicing the case in the newspapers."

Before sitting down again a moment later, Cotter said that Hoar's request was based "on no principle of law" and that he would therefore "spend no time answering it."

French, who had managed to maintain his composure, rose to say that, if the judges hesitated, even for a moment, in deciding against allowing the jury to hear the proposed testimony, he would ask to be allowed to cite cases that contradicted the district attorney's argument. Judge Colt assured him that this would be unnecessary because he and Judge Webb had already come to a decision regarding Nicklas, which they would announce in the morning.

At the start of trial the next day, the judges made quick work of Hoar's request, briefly ruling that the evidence Nicklas was prepared to present "has no logical bearing upon the issue we are now trying," and therefore his testimony would be inadmissible.

Agreeing with Cotter that the government had so far put on a weak case, court observers saw the ruling as a blow to any chances for a conviction Hoar may once have had. However, Hoar had as yet to conclude his case, and among his witnesses were the last two *Fuller* men not already heard from.

Sailor Oscar Andersson had nothing to say that others had not said already, but Frank Loheac, the Frenchman, testified that, shortly after being ordered by Bram to ring four bells at two o'clock, which was the signal for him to relieve Brown at the wheel, he saw Bram dart into and out of the forward companionway. Then a half-minute later, Loheac said he saw Monks emerge on deck and tell Bram, "Come down!"

Loheac then said he could distinctly hear gurgling noises coming from inside the afterhouse and, through the skylight on its roof, could see Monks change into his pants and shirt by the light of the main cabin swinging lantern, which had been taken down and moved to the chart-room floor.

Under cross-examination by Cotter, Loheac confirmed that Brown had told him the story about shooting a man in Rotterdam and getting off on a plea of insanity. Loheac also confirmed that he saw and heard all of the strange things Brown said and did—talking to himself, saying how easy it would be set the vessel afire, looking over the sides as if to jump, and so forth—that made the men suspect him of the murders.

Finally, Loheac confirmed that the wheel of the *Herbert Fuller* could be lashed, and for a time the vessel would still sail straight. In fact, Loheac said he had even seen Captain Nash doing this.

After a short recess, Hoar called his next witness, Dr. Frank W. Draper, coroner for Suffolk County (in which Boston resides), and someone who by his own count had conducted 1,022 autopsies and examined 4,680 cases of violent death.

Led by Hoar, the doctor proceeded to offer his opinion on all the gruesome aspects associated with the killing of Captain Nash, from the effects of the blows, to the sound the ax would have made on the skull, to the length of time until death, to the coagulation of spilled blood.

Cotter objected at almost every turn, complaining that the doctor was merely speculating on things the jurors could just as competently speculate on themselves and that the doctor claimed expertise in areas where he had no business doing so. For example, at one point when Hoar asked the witness if the captain's assailant could have avoided being splattered with blood, Cotter interrupted, "As a medical man, we don't question his qualifications, but as to the use of an ax, I submit that he hasn't had any more experience than a woodchopper."

In addressing Cotter's objection, Webb allowed Dr. Draper to answer a modified version of the question, and the answer was, yes, an assailant swinging an ax would not necessarily receive "blood upon his person or clothing."

When the doctor, who also held forth on other subjects, such as the causes of nausea and the cleaning of soiled shirts, finally left the stand, Hoar announced that the government's case had ended. With more than an hour left before five o'clock, Colt called for a short recess, after which he said the defense could begin its opening arguments. Citing the great physical strain placed on them during this long trial, however, French begged that he and Cotter be allowed to postpone their opening this until the morning. The judges agreed.

CHAPTER 9

Asa French, looking somewhat revived, stood before the jurors and forcefully began the opening argument for the defense. He criticized to the point of dismissal all the evidence the government had introduced against the man in the prisoner's dock but saved his most scathing remarks for the government's complete reliance on a single and, in his opinion, unreliable witness.

"We do not believe that conscientious, intelligent men, alive to the responsibility of the oaths which you have taken," French thundered, "would send a fellow human being to the gallows upon the evidence of such a man as Brown. If that be possible, neither you nor I nor anybody in the community would be safe for a single moment. Let me refer, because it is extraordinary, to the language used by the learned district attorney in his opening in reference to this witness."

French then read to the jurors something Hoar had told them on the first day of trial:

> I have been all through this case, and there is no question that in some people's minds there is a lurking suspicion that this man [Brown] at the wheel here had a hand in this murder. I claim first that he did not. I claim second that, if he did, he was simply part and parcel of the man [Bram] who sits in the dock over there and that he could not have committed a murder unless that man with him was also an accomplice.

"Gentlemen, that is a most extraordinary proposition," French remarked. "His principal witness, the witness upon whose testimony this case rests or falls, at the very outset is branded with suspicion by the district attorney in the language to which I have called to your attention.

"The question before you is not, Who killed Charles I. Nash? but, Did Thomas M. Bram kill him?"

If they could not determine this, French said, as men of conscience they had no choice but to "free the prisoner from his chains."

Pointing to Bram, French urged, "But gentleman, if upon all the evidence which you have heard, you can for a moment believe beyond a rational doubt that that man went down into that cabin on that night and committed those fiendish crimes, if you are prepared to believe that now, we ask you to reserve your judgment until you have seen him face to face and heard his voice and looked into his eyes upon that stand. We ask you to wait until he has subjected himself to the trying examination of the learned district attorney and the still greater searching power of your eyes. And then, gentlemen, when you have seen him and when you have heard him, when you have compared his story with that of the witnesses who have gone before, then we believe you will be able to judge him justly."

French's opening arguments continued for another hour and forty minutes, and at its conclusion the junior counsel for the defense appeared thoroughly drained and exhausted. Then, in a raspy voice that threatened to give out entirely, French quoted Polonius in *Hamlet*:

> To your ownselves be true,
> And it shall follow as the night the day,
> Thou cans't not then be false to any man.

Taking over from his junior partner (who, after his opening oration, looked to be near collapse), Cotter rose and said dramatically, "Let the defendant step out of the dock." The door to the dock was opened, and Bram walked with rapid and lengthy strides to the witness stand. It was the first occasion since the trial began that the accused was without Deputy Marshal Waters at his side, and a reporter noted, "Bram's newfound freedom seemed to have an inspiriting effect on him, and as he held his hand high in the air, while being sworn, the sight was certainly impressive."

That Cotter and French had decided to not only put Bram on the stand but also to make him their first witness came as a shock to legal observers. According to their collective wisdom, whatever good the defense might get out of an examination of the defendant would be totally undone by the prosecution's cross-examination. The tactic seemed risky, even reckless, and those adroit enough to have found a spectator's seat in the courtroom that day eagerly anticipated the outcome.

For Bram, it would be the first time he would tell his story in a court of law, and he appeared eager to do so.

Questioned by Cotter, the defendant said he was born in Dieppe Bay, Saint Kitts, to a British mother and a "Hollander" father and by age twelve was already working on vessels trading along the coast. Then, at age fifteen and unbeknownst to his mother (whom he hadn't seen since), he shipped as a sailor on the schooner *James A. Brown* bound for New York. Once there, he immediately signed as an ordinary seaman on a schooner in the sardine trade and had spent a year in the trade before finding work as a waiter in one of Mr. Dennett's restaurants in New York.

A few months and several promotions later, Bram said the owner sent him to Boston to manage the Dennett's at 239 Washington Street, which he did for about a year. Having just gotten married, he and his wife lived as lodgers on Thorndike Street in East Cambridge, but the situation, Bram explained, was not to her liking. They then moved back to New York, where he managed a newly opened Dennett's for about six months, during which time he was also involved with Christian missions in the city. Then Bram said he transferred to a Dennett's in Chicago, but this lasted just three months, and again he was back in New York managing yet another Dennett's, this one in the Bowery.

When Mr. Dennett fell into financial difficulty, Bram said, he was able to raise enough funds to buy the restaurant from him. However, it did not work out: "I stayed there a little while, and I couldn't make the business pay, the rental was too enormous, and the trade fell off, and I hadn't the means to keep it up, so I sold the place out for what I could get for it and paid the people I borrowed the money from, and with that I went to sea. That was in the year of eighty-eight."

Bram testified that he had followed the sea ever since, being mate or captain of the schooners *Henry M. Clark*, *Twilight*, *China*, *Cyrus Hall*, *William A. Drury*, and *Nellie Lamper*, along with the little brig *High-*

lander and the barkentine *White Wings*. In some of these vessels, he had an ownership stake, such as the *China*, which, Bram said, suffered distress in Belize (Cotter let mention of this incident pass). Bram explained that his many voyages took him as far away as South America and England, but in between this ocean odyssey, his father-in-law secured employment for him with the New York Lighter and Transportation Company.

Bram explained that he stayed with that firm about two and a half years before going off to sea again, signing aboard different ships, including the *Cestrian*, the steamer that landed him in Boston in June of this year. Bram explained that he found his position as mate aboard the *Herbert Fuller* on the recommendation of a Mr. Parker of the ship chandlery store on Commercial Street. Unlike the second mate and the six sailors who joined the *Herbert Fuller* at Long Wharf a day before departure, Bram said Nash had hired him almost a month earlier, June 7, as the barkentine was being readied for the trip to Rosario.

Bram added that, when he met Monks for the first time, he told him, "If you have got any more baggage than you can accommodate in your room, I have got plenty of room underneath my bed; you can put your baggage there."

Cotter made some general inquiries about the loading of the barkentine and the first part of the voyage before asking Bram about the orders Nash had given regarding the sixth day under sail, Monday, July 13.

Bram said that, as usual, Nash had given the orders for that day the night before, and those were that the crew take sand and canvas to the afterdeck and the exterior of the afterhouse. Bram said he put the men to work bright and early, five thirty, the next morning and that, when he told the sailor Brown to use both hands, Brown complied but remarked, "Is this good enough for you?"

On Monday night, Bram said that he had the first "dog watch." Interrupting, Cotter asked what *dog watch* meant, and in answering, Bram got his first of many opportunities to discuss all things nautical.

"It separates both watches from having the same watch every night," explained Bram. "Instead of having four hours through every night, we divide the four-to-eight watch into two watches; the starboard watch takes two hours from four to six, and the port watch, or whatever watch it is, takes the watch from six to eight. We had the port watch, my watch from six to eight—the dog watch."

Resuming with his narrative of events, Bram said that, when his dog watch was over, he went below to his room and remained there until about twelve o'clock, when Blomberg, standing in the forward companionway, called his name.

"The second mate asked me if I wanted a drink. Says I, 'Where did you get it?' He says, 'Oh, the passenger gave it to me.' And with that he had a little flask and tin cup, the top of a dinner pail that those workmen carry around. And he drained the contents of a bottle in this tin cup, which was a very small one, and he gave it to me, and I drank it. He throwed the tin cup and the bottle away overboard, and he went below. I then started to pace the deck between the mizzen and mainmasts, sometimes athwartships and sometimes fore and aft."

At around one in the morning, Bram said, he went below to his room for a sandwich that Spencer had earlier prepared for him and also to have a drink of whiskey. Referring to a diagram of the deck, Bram said that he then went above to see that Loheac had been relieved from the lookout by Perdok.

"The lookout?" asked Cotter referring to the diagram.

"Yes, sir. Forward here, on the topgallant forecastle. During the hour from twelve until one, Henry Perdok was stationed about here, just abaft this forward house, on the deck load to windward, and I was walking, as I said before, between the main and mizzenmasts. From one until two o'clock, I spent the better part of my time leeward, just abaft the main topmast backstay."

"What do you mean by that term?" asked Cotter who, being a landlubber, was having trouble understanding Bram's seafaring jargon.

"Well, the vessel was on the starboard tack," Bram answered, "and I stationed myself right abaft this topmast backstay here, sitting on top of a temporary rail that we had built on top of the deck load, which stood about six feet high, it was made of three-by-four pieces of scantling. [I was] facing forward and of course right abreast of the beam here, looking for vessels coming up to leeward, because anything coming up to leeward would have the right of way."

"So, approaching vessels would go on which side of your vessel?"

"Well they would be coming up under our lee, so of course it may be necessary to keep off if we were too close to them, but if they were far enough to windward, we would not have to do anything."

Cotter, who may or may not have gotten all of this straight, said, "Very well, now you can continue."

Bram said that he remained sitting on the lee rail watching for vessels when, "very close to two o'clock, possibly a couple of minutes, I don't know the time, I heard a noise aft here on the deck load. This part of the load I stored myself; it was only dunnage."

"What do you mean by dunnage?" queried Cotter.

"Some small stuff, a part of the load the captain bought for his own personal use. A part of the cargo, it was not a cargo; it was for the vessel's use, dunnage, that I stored along this alleyway, myself and the second mate, and it was not stored properly. Every time one walks along here, the lumber makes a noise because it is stored uneven. At about a couple of minutes before two o'clock, I heard this noise behind me, and I got up and looked around, and I seen a man about abreast of this mizzen peak jig."

Cotter skipped the opportunity to have Bram define *mizzen peak jig* and instead had him continue.

Bram said that the man he saw there was Brown and that, as he, Bram, got up from the rail to walk aft to check the time by the clock on the wall above the table in the main cabin, Brown was already returning to the wheel. Bram remembered that he then ducked down into the open entrance of the forward companionway and, without having to enter the afterhouse, saw that the clock read two o'clock, meaning it was time for Loheac to take the wheel.

"I sung out to Brown, 'Four bells,' and shaking my hand at the same time. I got no response. I turned around, and Frank Loheac came along here, and I said to him, 'Four bells.'

"He says, 'Four bells, sir.'

"And with that I walked around from the weather side to the lee side and went aft: came along this way [pointing to the diagram] and came up by Brown. When I got there, I saw Brown stooping down, putting his slippers on, and he got up when I got there, putting his hand on the wheel, and I went back to windward here. At that time Frank Loheac relieved him, and Brown went forward, and in going forward he took a bucket out of this rack. We had a bucket rack stood along here [pointing to the diagram] that held about half a dozen buckets on the afterpart of this afterhouse, and he went forward with it."

Bram testified that he left Loheac at the wheel and, like Brown had just done, also went forward. When he was between the main- and mizzenmasts, Bram said he looked back and saw a figure standing in the forward companionway pointing a revolver, its barrel shining in what little moonlight there was, right at him.

"And seeing the revolver, I didn't hesitate. I picked up a piece of board that was standing there by the mainsheet and held the board in front of me in this way. When I came up, Mr. Monks says, 'Who is that?' Says I, 'It is me.' He says, 'Come down here, Mr. Bram, don't be afraid. It is me; the captain is killed.' Says I, 'What?' and with the scare, I let the board drop, and it went right down the steps to the bottom of the companionway."

Bram added that he and Monks went into the main cabin, where they took down the swinging lantern, turned it up "full blast," and made their way into the chart room and then into the adjoining stateroom occupied by Monks. Bram recalled that they placed the lantern on the stateroom floor so Monks could change out of his pajamas and into a shirt and pants.

While Monks was changing, Bram said, he saw the captain on the carpet and heard him making a gurgling noise. Leaving Monks briefly, Bram said that he went over and touched the captain's feet; they were cold.

"When Monks got ready," Bram explained, "I says, 'Let's go into Mrs. Nash's room now, and see Mrs. Nash.' He says, 'It ain't no use going there. I have been there; she is dead already. Don't lose any time in this cabin; there are too many holes around.'"

Admitting to Cotter that he had been just as scared as was Monks, Bram said they left the lantern, still lit, where they had placed it on the floor and hastily exited the afterhouse by way of the forward companionway. When they reached the top of the deck load, Bram said that they then went forward, where they stationed themselves amidships, near the mizzenmast rigging.

Then, Bram explained, "I, thinking of the sight I had just seen down in the cabin, I got sick to my stomach, throwed up a little, close to where I was. And Monks and I stood there, and said I, 'Mr. Monks, this is very funny.'

"Monks said to me, 'Where is the second mate?'

"Says I, 'Ain't he in his room?'

"He said, 'I didn't see him.'

"'Well,' I said, 'if he is not down there, he is forward with the men. Monks, let us go forward and wake the steward up. I think it is better to get someone else with us than to be alone.'

"Said he, 'We will wait until daylight and call the steward. Don't move here because it ain't safe.'"

Bram then related how, at first light, they woke Spencer and how Spencer, after hearing of the murders, requested that Bram give him his revolver.

"Where did you obtain the revolver?" Cotter asked.

"Oh, excuse me," Bram answered. "On my way up from the companionway from Monks's room. I said, 'Wait until I get my revolver,' and we stopped in my room, and I unlocked my trunk and took an old revolver that I had had for many years."

Bram's testimony continued. He explained that, on the morning after the crime, when all had finished examining the afterhouse interior, he had asked every man, including Monks and Brown, if they knew anything about what happened, and all had answered that they did not.

Bram said he declared, "If that is the case, I don't blame anybody for this occurrence. The people are dead, and they cannot answer for themselves, and God only knows how it occurred. As far as I know, I know nothing about it myself."

It was then, according to Bram, when the theory of the murders was introduced by Monks and Monks alone. After Monks had composed the written version of his theory, Bram said he protested the part, added by Monks as a postscript, about having been offered whiskey by the second mate at twelve midnight. It was this drink, according to Monks, that had made him throw up and act as if he had been drugged.

Questioned by Cotter, Bram said he signed the paper anyway because it was true that he had vomited, even if had nothing to do with the drink Blomberg had given him. Asked what had become of the vomit, Bram answered, "Well, to the best of my recollection about that, there was very little of this stuff, and whatever was said about this [to preserve a sample for analysis] was said after I slid into the stuff."

Next, Bram explained how, when they were all inspecting the afterhouse, Spencer noticed that the curtain in the chart-room window had been torn down and how, when seeing the condition of the captain's wife's nightgown, Spencer had declared, "It looks like someone has been interfering with Mrs. Nash."

At the burial in the jolly boat after Monks had done a little reading from the prayer book, Bram said he asked the gathering, "Are there any Masons among you?" When the answer was no, he had cried and repeated words that only a fellow Mason would understand.

Answering additional questions from Cotter, Bram described how Brown's odd and suspicious behavior, most notably his taking his clothes off and seeming ready to jump overboard midocean, led to his arrest. After Brown was tied to the mizzenmast, Bram said he went to see him and explained, "I was left alone with Brown then. He was then shaking and said to me, 'Did the passenger tell you he saw me kill those people?'

"Said I, 'The passenger said nothing to me, but your actions to everybody denotes it.' Said I, 'Who tore that curtain down in the cabin?'

"He said, 'I did,' and with that I got up and left him."

Bram testified that three days after Brown's arrest, Saturday afternoon, he went forward to the carpenter shop, where he kept his trunk that contained all of his clothes. Interrupting, Cotter asked, "Now, did you continue to wear the same articles of clothing until the Saturday after the murder?"

"Yes, sir, everything I had on. When I went into the carpenter shop," Bram continued, "I discovered that the trunk was open. The lock wasn't broken but pried open from the lower edge of the catch, where the lock catches. The steward was then resting right overhead of this carpenter shop, underneath the big boat, looking down into the carpenter shop. I turned to him and said, 'Steward, have you been down here to my trunk?'

"He told me then, 'No.'

"'It is very funny,' says I, 'my trunk is broken open.' I said no more about it."

Bram explained that he changed out of his old clothes and threw them up on deck, after which he took a pail of fresh water and, he explained, "put some gold dust in it for washing—a kind of pulverized stuff, like pearline."

Again interrupting, Cotter wanted to know, "Was that gold dust put there [by you] for the purpose of removing blood or anything of that kind?"

"No, sir. It was put there to take out dirt." Bram added that he allowed the clothes to soak overnight.

Continuing with his story, Bram said that it was about seven o'clock the next morning when Sable Island came into view, and knowing Halifax was near, he ordered the men to prepare the anchors.

There followed, Bram testified, the sighting of the Canadian tramp, and then at around noon, the "next thing I knew, the steward got me by the back of the throat here and throwed me down backwards." The witness also related such things as Spencer's obsession with salvage rights to the vessel.

Cotter then changed his line of inquiry and, apparently anticipating that Hoar would delve into the subject, had Bram explain that he had purchased whiskey for the voyage to Rosario but that at Long Wharf he had accidently spilled most of it. Cotter also got Bram to state that, whenever aboard a vessel, he only sipped a little whiskey, and then only at night.

Following these questions, the attorney had his client describe the workings of the *Herbert Fuller* at sea. This Bram did in such a treatise-like manner that it likely became tedious for some to listen to but apparently not for Judge Webb, who must have had seawater in his veins.

From the bench, Webb would frequently interrupt Bram to ask him about this or that nautical point, and then, as if they were the only two people in the courtroom, witness and justice would discuss the matter at length. Seeing that the court clock was nearing five, Cotter sought to tie up some loose ends.

He had Bram testify that, in choosing between making port in French Cayenne or in Halifax, he had chosen the former because, due to the trade winds, it was actually the faster sail, but because all the other men wanted Halifax, that's where he headed. Bram also testified that the reason all but one of the cartridges in his revolver were nicked and useless—as Spencer had discovered—was because the revolver, already old when given to him years ago by a sea captain, only "sometimes" worked.

Bram emphasized, however, that, except for test firing the gun, "I never used the revolver and had no use for it."

Finally, Cotter wanted to know how long the *Herbert Fuller* could run with the wheel lashed. "Well, probably ten or fifteen minutes," Bram answered. "Twenty minutes sometimes."

Cotter resumed his examination the next morning, minus the help of French, who evidently needed to recuperate from his oratory of the day before.

Cotter asked the defendant questions about how the *Herbert Fuller* had navigated between the time it left Nantasket Roads to the day of the murders (by compass only, Bram answered), the purpose of the logbook (mainly to record damages for insurance purposes), and if the logbook had been maintained after he was put in irons (it had not).

As to Brown, Cotter asked, "Did you notice any peculiarity about Brown?"

"Well, only he had a bad habit of speaking to himself and making motions."

"You may describe the motions."

"He squared off as if he was fighting with somebody."

Here, Bram demonstrated by raising his fists and moving his head side to side, as if to dodge imaginary blows. When Cotter asked about Brown speaking to himself, Bram recalled that, one or two days before the murders, Brown had been speaking to himself so loudly that he had to be told to stop. Cotter then showed Bram a copy of the deposition that Ingraham claimed Bram had signed as "A. Bram" in Halifax. In looking at the signature, however, Bram testified that the handwriting was not his and that additionally he never signed his name "A. Bram."

Finally, Cotter asked point-blank, "Mr. Bram, did you have anything to do with taking the lives of any of the three persons whose lives were lost that night?"

"Nothing whatever, sir."

"Did you have an understanding, directly or indirectly, with anybody in regard to that deed?"

"Nothing at all. No one knew nothing about it, sir."

It was now ten thirty in the morning, and the trial was in its twelfth day. Hoar, Cotter's opposing counsel, would get a chance to do something that he probably doubted he would ever get to do: cross-examine Bram.

CHAPTER 10

The district attorney began his cross-examination by having the defendant relate, in detail and at length, nearly every single aspect (it seemed) of his personal history: his birth in 1864; his arrival in New York in 1879; his marriage in 1886 or '87 (Bram couldn't recall which); his US naturalization in 1888; and the names and captains of all the vessels he had ever sailed on and their cargoes, plus what wages he had been paid.

Hoar also tried to probe into the *White Wings* allegations made by Nicklas, but Cotter's objection was sustained by the judges. Hoar then focused on Bram's marriage and domestic troubles. The defendant admitted that there had been "little differences" between himself and his wife, but as far as he knew, she had not divorced him since they last saw each other. Next, Hoar questioned Bram on his Methodism, his work for Dennett's, and of living in Nova Scotia and commanding vessels from there. It was his time in Nova Scotia, Bram explained, that led him to consider himself a Nova Scotian. Lastly, the district attorney asked the defendant how it was that he had come to Boston around June 1 prior to signing with Nash on June 10 of this year.

Bram replied that he had been in Liverpool after leaving the steamer *Manning*, on which he served as mate for a voyage to Buenos Aires, and "I wanted to get back home" to Brooklyn to visit his wife and children, whom he had not seen for a year. This was early May, and in Liverpool the only vessel in port headed in the general direction of New York was the steamer *Cestrian*, about to embark on a round trip to Boston. There being no officer's vacancies on the steamer, Bram said he signed papers "as a sailor before the mast" just to get across the Atlantic. Then, when the *Cestrian* docked in Boston and when no one was looking, Bram said that he walked off the ship "in broad daylight" and did not return.

The trap set, Hoar pounced, "On the *Cestrian* what did you get?"

"I don't know what the pay was."

"You did not get it, did you?"

"No, I shipped to get back home."

"What did you do here?"

"I stayed here."

"You deserted, didn't you?"

"I walked off and left her."

"That is the reason you did not get any pay, is it not?"

"Certainly," Bram confirmed, adding that because of this he didn't have money enough to leave Boston and see his family in New York.

Having failed in his first attempt to trap Bram, Hoar set another one. How was it, Hoar asked, he had come aboard the *Herbert Fuller* the last day it was on Long Wharf with just $28.25 to his name, yet that very same day he was able to loan a man from his boardinghouse money?

"I gave him twenty-five cents," answered Bram.

Changing the subject, Hoar asked how it was that Bram came aboard the *Herbert Fuller* shortly before its departure with a supply of whiskey. Bram explained that the whiskey, in a two-gallon jug, was intended for an acquaintance in South America, a man named Juan Demazir, who lived somewhere along the Paraguayan River. And, Hoar wanted to know, what had become of the whiskey? Bram answered that, while loading his things aboard the *Herbert Fuller*, he had rested the jug on a scantling atop the deck load of lumber, but the wake from a passing tug knocked the jug onto its side. The cork popped out, and by the time he realized what had happened, there were just two quarts left.

Hoar asked, "What did you put the two quarts in?"

"I put one quart in a bottle that I got from the steward."

"One of those flat bottles, flat white bottles?"

"Like a medicine bottle, yes."

"With the sides flaring up and flat on the ends and with a curved top?"

"That is right, yes, sir. That is right."

Interrupting, Cotter said to Hoar, "You appear to understand it."

"I appear to understand that kind of bottle," Hoar replied and then proceeded to ask Bram what he did with the remaining quart. Bram said he kept it in the jug because Spencer had no more medicine bottles to lend.

Having extracted from the defendant whatever it was he had intended to extract regarding the whiskey, Hoar then inquired about the drink of liquor the second mate, Blomberg, had given the defendant on July 14 at twelve midnight, less than two hours before the murders.

In his earlier examination Cotter had touched on this odd episode, but under Hoar's cross-examination the episode only seemed odder.

Bram testified that Blomberg had poured the liquor from a small glass flask and into a little metal cup of the type that formed the top part of a dinner pail. Bram, however, admitted that there were no dinner pails around at the time, and in fact, he never saw a dinner pail while on the *Herbert Fuller*. According to Bram, there was not enough liquor in the flask for the two of them, but Bram said, "He told me he had a drink; he told me he had his drink."

"Then what did you do with that cup?" asked Hoar.

"I drank it, sir. I drank the liquor."

"Did you take the flask in your hands and pour it, or did he pour it?"

"No, sir. The second mate done that himself."

"And then what did he do with the—"

"He throwed it overboard."

"What?"

"The flask and the cup."

"And the cup, both?"

"Yes, sir."

Bram explained that he had another drink an hour later, at one o'clock. This time, though, he was alone in his stateroom, and the drink, taken in a little glass, was some of what remained in his two-gallon whiskey jug. The reason he later vomited on deck in the presence of Monks, Bram explained, was not due to anything he drank but because of the sandwich prepared by Spencer that he ate not long before the passenger beckoned him into the afterhouse, where he saw Nash lying on the carpet.

"The condition that the captain was in. I got sick to my stomach and throwed up a very little on the weather side."

Bram insisted that the theory Blomberg had put something in the liquor came from the passenger: "I never mentioned a word about being drugged, sir, to Mr. Monks."

Under further questioning by Hoar and while holding the large model of the *Herbert Fuller* and using a pencil to pinpoint the exact location on the deck load where he had vomited, Bram explained that at daylight he, Monks, and Spencer came upon the bile and "to the best of my recollection my feet slipped some way or other under me, and I remember the slippers that I had on got into this little bit of stuff. We stood on the deck there then, and there was nothing more said about it to my knowledge, about analyzation or nothing else."

Bram was also adamant that, when Monks was changing out of his pajamas, he had never left the passenger's stateroom door except to quickly check on Captain Nash and that he was never told by Monks to "come back and stay here."

Hoar asked, "Why didn't you undertake to do something for the captain?"

"The captain laid there cold. He looked like dead. He appeared to be."

"But he was breathing?"

"Once or twice this noise [demonstrating]. Once or twice when Mr. Monks and I was down there. About twice I think."

"Did you undertake to offer him any assistance at all?"

"The captain was helpless then. He was then—I think he was dead. Mr. Monks, he said he was dead, and he appeared to be. His feet were cold."

"Did you get near enough to see how he was cut in any way?"

"No, sir, not then."

Hoar's questions led Bram to say he had wanted to check on the captain's wife, telling Monks as they passed her stateroom on the way out of the afterhouse, "Let us go into Mrs. Nash's room." But Monks had objected, saying, "No use going in there, for I have been in there already, and she is dead."

Bram also denied having had more than the liquor Blomberg gave him at midnight and the "ordinary" drink of whiskey he poured himself an hour later. Additionally, and in contradiction to Monks's testimony, Bram said that once up on deck he did not "stagger at all," that Monks never slapped him on the back, and that Monks never told him to "brace up."

Focusing on the lantern, Hoar returned to the period when Bram and Monks were in the afterhouse to allow Monks to change from his pajamas. Bram had given several explanations about why he left lantern in the passenger's cabin, such as because it was safer in the darkness on deck.

Demanded Hoar, "Now, what do you give for your final reason for not taking that lamp out from that cabin?"

"Well, at the time that Mr. Monks and I went down there, I was so perplexed, and so was Mr. Monks himself, for what reason I cannot really explain. I cannot justify myself in doing it, no sir, because at that moment it was a very hard thing to tell what to do or what I did do."

Why, Hoar asked, had Bram not had the courage to return to the afterhouse to see for himself about Mrs. Nash after he had moved Monks topside?

"Yes, sir, that is easily explained."

"Explain it."

"This was about two o'clock at night on the deck. I was alone on deck and aroused with what happened back in the captain's cabin. The only man with me at this time was Mr. Monks. He was anything but in a right steady state of mind. He was not better than I was at this time. We went to his room and got sufficient clothes and came on deck. When I make a suggestion [to check on Mrs. Nash], he objects. Well now, I would not feel justified in going anywhere aboard that ship alone out of sight of Mr. Monks."

"Why?"

"For the simple reason I was scared myself."

"A boy not twenty-one years of age, and you say you were trembling?"

"He was as bad as I was."

The district attorney's cross-examination was truncated by the end of the court day, and the twelve jurors were escorted back to their lodgings in the Quincy House, where a Christmas Eve dinner awaited them.

Although neither judges nor attorneys for either side were averse to holding court on Christmas Day, the legality of doing so was unclear, and so on Christmas the jurors enjoyed a carriage ride through the suburbs. The next morning at nine thirty, however, the twelve were back in their box to listen.

As before, the district attorney delved deeply into the defendant's background while also trying to find contradictions between the defendant's testimony and those of the other witnesses. As before, the defendant held his own, even to the point of becoming cocky.

Bram would interrupt the district attorney: "Aren't you getting a little mixed, Mr. Hoar?"

He would correct him: "Pardon me, you are making a mistake."

He would instruct him: "Let me straighten the matter out for you."

He would criticize him: "You are speaking of too many things at the same time."

And he would caution him: "We had better be careful because we may get these things mixed up, Mr. Hoar."

All day long the sparring continued, with Hoar trying desperately to find a crack in Bram's story that could be turned into a chasm and Bram giving him no satisfaction. Bram had a cogent explanation for everything. For example, after the murders but before he was put in irons, Bram had made some notes based on the ship's log on loose-leaf stationery. Hoar, trying to make this appear as suspicious as possible, asked Bram why. Bram calmly explained that a vessel's log always stayed with the vessel and that, should the *Herbert Fuller* sail away after it reached shore, its log would do likewise. Therefore, Bram said, he wanted to record the condition of the white pine during the voyage, which he could later show Mr. Shepard, owner of the cargo.

The following morning, Hoar announced that he was done with the witness. His cross-examination had lasted nearly ten hours, and spectator Grinnell, who had sat through all of it, summed up the defendant and his performance:

> Bram was of average height and had a habit of standing erect with his shoulders thrown far back. He was very alert. His naturally dark complexion was darkened by exposure. When his face was quiet, it had a solid, businesslike look—quite calculating. But when he spoke, a strange mixture of qualities was disclosed. His voice was very resounding. Everyone could hear him everywhere. When speaking to a friend, his black eyes would shine and sparkle, he would show his white teeth under his thick lips and would put his hand in a persuasive manner on the person to whom he was talking. But when he was

> under cross-examination, his eye became steadily fixed and hard to a startling degree, his mouth grew confidently firm, and he carried his head in a way that brought into prominence a very long underjaw. His manner, when questioned about the murders, was that of doing a piece of business that he must attend to very carefully and which was wearing everybody but himself. He testified with the air of quite willingly delivering a lecture upon a subject which no one knew anything but himself, and he knew everything. He was very [polite] to his cross-examiner. His nerve, coolness, and power of endurance made him apparently the freshest man in the courtroom at the end of day after day. And his presence and conciliatory habit were so effective that many spectators who believed him guilty were sure that twelve men would not find such a smooth talker guilty of such a crime as murder.

Bram had proved that he was more than a "smooth talker." At Hoar's expense, Bram showed he could make the courtroom erupt into laughter.

At one point Hoar had asked, "Were you in the longitude of Cayenne when you changed the course on the day after the murders?"

"Yes, sir."

"And you were in the latitude of Cayenne also?"

"If we were, we would have been in Cayenne, sir."

When Hoar questioned Bram's fear that, while he was on deck with Monks just after the murders, an unknown assailant might be lurking under the long boat stored on top of the forward house, Hoar asked Bram, "How did you expect anybody could come out of that boat to attack you?"

"The same way he got in."

Apparently pleased with how he had acquitted himself on the stand, once back in his prisoner's dock, Bram appeared to be in fine spirits, grinning and nodding to Cotter and French and even playfully slapping his ever-present guard, Deputy Marshal Walters, on the shoulder. Bram also seemed pleased with the final witnesses that Cotter and French called to the stand in his defense.

Two were expert "alienists," what today would be called psychiatrists, who diagnosed Charles Brown as "suffering from mania or a species of insanity," and another was Captain Martin A. M. Humphreys, a seafarer since age fifteen and now a "lad" of seventy-four summers.

Humphreys, described by a reporter as a "modest-appearing man of mild demeanor," was called by the defense to verify that the *Herbert Fuller* could have had its wheel lashed and still stay on course for an extended period of time.

Taking over from Cotter, French asked, "What experience have you had, Captain?"

"I once saw a man leave the wheel of a vessel of which I was master, certainly not less than half an hour. There was a mutiny onboard, and the sailors were shooting at me. I shot four of them, and we put one in irons."

There was a collective gasp in the courtroom, and the modest-appearing man of mild demeanor left the stand.

In all, French called up eight veteran seafarers, each of the old salts swearing an oath on the Bible that a full-rigged ship such as the *Herbert Fuller* could stay on course for ten, fifteen, twenty, thirty, or even sixty minutes with its wheel unattended. One witness, Captain John Wynmiatt, stated that he had once been at a wheel two hours "without putting a hand to it."

Cotter's remaining witnesses included Edwards K. Barker, a clerk at the ship chandler's store at 196 Commercial Street, and Hugh G. Messenger, a ship carpenter of East Boston. The clerk testified that his store had cashed a note for Bram last July, some of which Bram had used to purchase clothing; he chose to leave the remaining nine dollars as store credit (a choice, Cotter presumably would have argued, hardly reflective of a man who was money-mad).

The carpenter testified that he had traveled to Halifax and boarded the *Herbert Fuller* on August 7 and 8 to make measurements and that it was impossible to both keep both hands on the wheel and look through the after-cabin window. Even with one hand on the wheel, he testified, and leaning forward to the utmost possible extent, all that could be seen was a little light from the cabin.

Hoar spent much of the morning during the next day of trial, the fourteenth, December 30, presenting his own two expert alienists, who were positive that Brown's actions in Rotterdam were not those of an insane man. Hoar, though, was denied the opportunity to have his own weathered mariners testify that a wheel could not be left unattended because Cotter pointed out that, with Brown's testimony earlier, the prosecution had already closed its argument on that point.

Hoar was, however, allowed to recall Monks. He aimed to undercut Bram's assertion that, while down in the afterhouse with Monks, Monks had ever said, "There is no use in going into Mrs. Nash's room, for I have been in there already, and she is dead."

Taking the stand once again and looking none too happy about it, the young man told Hoar that he had never uttered those or similar words. Monks said he had waited until they had left the afterhouse to tell Bram that Mrs. Nash was dead.

When it was his turn to question Monks, Cotter, not pleased with this answer, walked to within a few feet of the witness stand and, pointing his finger at the young man's face, asked, "Why did you not tell Bram that Mrs. Nash was dead, as well as the captain, when you went on deck [the first time] with a loaded weapon and pointed at him, Mr. Monks? Why did you not tell him that she was dead when he went downstairs with you and to your room? Why did you not tell him while you were changing your clothes; when he was with you in the room; and never until, as your say, you were on deck a second time?"

After a pause, Monks replied, "I was in a good deal of a hurry to get my clothes on and get on deck."

"Were you in such a hurry you could not tell him?"

"I don't know."

Stepping even closer to the witness stand, and in his most insinuating manner, Cotter stated as much as asked, "There are some things about this case and what took place that night that you don't remember, Mr. Monks. Are there not, Mr. Monks?"

"Yes, sir."

One of the first and, it turned out, the last witness in the trial to testify, Monks left the stand.

The judges then announced there would be a recess, after which Cotter would begin his closing argument for the defense. It was also announced that the district attorney, in a tacit admittance that the money trail had led nowhere, requested jurors to disregard all testimony regarding Bram's pay and savings.

News that Cotter was soon to launch into the oration that might determine if Bram lived or hanged caused so much excitement that, to mollify the usual crowd of would-be spectators in the hallway outside, the court doors were thrown open to offer the masses a view.

Cotter rose to address the jurors and, practically leaning over the rail of the jurors' box and in a voice so soft it was difficult for those, save his immediate audience, to discern, said, "We are here, Mr. Foreman and gentlemen, in doing that which is right between man and man, between the United States and the defendant . . . aiding in the administration of justice, Mr. Foreman and gentleman—that attribute of divinity which is preexistent of all earthly things, eternal and immutable. Its authority is founded on the act of God speaking to the heart, which faith has purified, and to the mind of intelligence, which experience had endowed with intelligence to understand. That is what you are to deal with."

Cotter continued that they, as jurors, were only to determine beyond a reasonable doubt if the accused committed the murder of Charles Nash: "That is the issue, the only issue. And you are not called upon to go forward. You are not called upon to say what the probabilities are, what the possibilities are. The government takes its position. The government must prove everything that is material to that allegation, and until these allegations are proven by the overwhelming hand of testimony, Thomas M. Bram in the eyes of the law is as innocent as any man in your panel. . . . If he is guilty, you say guilty. That means disgrace, ignominious death, a felon's grave. If not guilty, it means life, radiant with hopes and with future prospects."

With these and similar exhortations that justice be done, Cotter prepared the twelve men for their awesome responsibility, and then Cotter turned his attention to the passenger, Lester Monks, who Cotter said emerged from the afterhouse at around two o'clock on the morning of the murders and pointed a revolver at the mate Thomas Bram, who was then at his post of duty, walking from one side of the deck to the other near the mizzenmast. Cotter reminded the jurors that Bram's reaction—which was to pick up a piece of plank and then to either throw it or drop it—upon seeing a man in the dark with a revolver pointing at him was of no importance. The prosecution admitted as much, Cotter reminded them.

Hoar rose to object, but Cotter stopped him and noted that, if Hoar now thought it was important, he could say so in his own closing argument. Allowed to continue, Cotter said, "What next? He [Bram] responds to Mr. Monks's call. He accompanies Mr. Monks to the cabin—and there, there is an issue. There are other issues in this case, Mr. Foreman and gentlemen, and I will have occasion to say to you that the testimony of Mr. Monks is not entitled to credence, that he has been shifting his position."

Continuing with his attack against Monks (and referring to testimony given earlier but since lost to the record), Cotter declared, "He was ready to lay this crime on the shoulders of any man onboard of that vessel. He charged the crime to the second mate; he charged the crime to Brown; he charged the crime and suspected Henry Slice—and after charging the second mate and charging Brown and suspecting Slice."

And then, Cotter asked, what did Monks do when he got ashore?

"The moment he strikes Halifax, he is under the advice of counsel; his statement is prepared by counsel; his father and his uncle and other distinguished people are present before the American consul. He is the only person who acts under the advice of counsel, the only person whom counsel is assisting.

"For what purpose? Charged with no offense, charged with no crime, and the counsel selected by him undertakes to cross-examine Mr. Bram and to fasten this offense upon Bram!"

Referring to Lester Monks and his father and uncle and his attorney Forbes, Cotter continued, "They come to Boston, and what follows? The Halifax counsel comes here and is aiding and assisting [Hoar] before the US commissioner in a prosecution against Brown and Bram.

"Monks, under the advice, before the district attorney and elsewhere, of legal counsel, is here, and no charge is made against him. He is not the defendant. But all this time he is apprehensive that a charge will be made and that he must be protecting himself. To protect himself he feels that it is incumbent upon him to convict and to condemn somebody, and from the time that vessel struck Halifax until the present moment, Lester H. Monks and his influence and his counsel are aiding in this prosecution and endeavoring to convict the prisoner at the bar.

"We are not charging him [Monks] with any offense; we are not charging him with taking any life—even though our client did say that it was singular, and I repeat, Mr. Foreman and gentlemen, that my client was justified in saying it was singular, that this man should occupy an apartment with only a frail partition between him and Captain Nash on one side and Mrs. Nash on the other side; a doorway leading from his apartment to either room, whether locked or unlocked; the second mate's room only a few feet away, and that these three people, these three persons, were chopped, battered, with marks on the ceiling and on the partitions, on the one side and the other of this man, and he was never aroused, never heard the occurrence, until it was all over with and he heard the cry of a woman. He went on deck with a revolver in his hand and the captain's revolver under his mattress. Bram was justified in saying, 'It is singular he doesn't know more about this occurrence than what he has told.'"

Demonstrating the hidden hand that the Monks family still had in the case, Cotter pointed out that Lester's father, Franklin, had attended every single day of the trial, including days when his son, the "young man who delighted in being called 'the Harvard student,' 'the hero of the occasion,' 'the gallant commander pro tem,'" was not even present.

Then, as he had earlier during his cross-examination of the Harvard student, Cotter ridiculed the idea that the "amusing" theory of the murders came from anybody other than the man who wrote it in the first person ("I went to bed," "My first recollections were these," "My theory of the tragedy is this," etc.) and who not once but twice had signed it "Lester Hawthorne Monks."

Said Cotter, "And yet he has the cowardice, the lack of manhood and of character, to come in here and try to swear away the life of, to prejudice a fellow being's life, on account of that paper."

Not long after Monks had written and endorsed his theory, Cotter argued, Monks had agreed with all the other men that the bizarre behavior Charley Brown exhibited both before and after the crimes indicated guilt. This resulted, Cotter said, in Brown's being charged.

"They charged him with murdering the three persons whose lives were lost onboard the *Herbert Fuller*. No suspicion rested upon the mate."

And in fact, Cotter said, the mate strove to maintain harmony among the men immediately after the murders, had made no objection when the men wanted to sail for Halifax instead of Cayenne, and as their new captain had faithfully navigated them to within one hundred miles of their new destination. But then, Cotter said, Spencer and the others began contemplating salvage rights.

Explained Cotter, "They discussed five hundred dollars apiece, Loheac said. Spencer said the matter of salvage was spoken of. It was also mentioned that, if the mate brought that vessel into port, the sailors would not be entitled to the salvage of five hundred dollars apiece, and on Sunday afternoon, five or six days after this tragedy, the mate was violently, without notice, seized by that crew, including Spencer and Loheac, aided and abetted by Monks."

It was only shortly before this, Cotter reminded, that the manacled Brown had suddenly stated, "I saw the mate do the offense. I had my hands on the wheel. I looked in the cabin window. I saw him swing the ax. I saw the captain fall."

Continuing, Cotter said that it was "on that testimony or that representation the man [Brown] who is charged with the offense cannot escape unless he involves somebody else, and on that representation Thomas M. Bram is suspected."

Cotter reminded jurors that Bram had not been charged with any crime by the Canadians but was held instead at the request of US consul Ingraham. By turning Bram over to Halifax detective Power, therefore, Ingraham had acted illegally, and Power had violated Bram's rights by stripping him, interrogating him, and seizing his clothing. The Halifax police had also violated Bram's rights by breaking into and searching his trunk.

Cotter retold the entire incident of Brown shooting at a man in Rotterdam, of being committed to a hospital, and of escaping all charges after being declared insane. He reminded jurors that Hoar held Brown as a codefendant between August and October until putting Brown (but never Bram) before a grand jury, implying that Brown had received favored treatment, and as a result, at trial he did Hoar's bidding.

As for Brown's testimony before them, Cotter told the jurors, "And I repeat that he was not a frank witness, that he was not a fair witness, that he knew more and could have answered more fully than he did on the first day he testified, that there was a deliberate attempt to evade our questions. And that, I submit to you, Mr. Foreman, and to every one of your associates, is a fair statement of the conduct of Charles Brown. And the fact that Charles Brown was put in a prisoner's cell and modified [his testimony] the following day is significant."

Cotter hammered home the point that, although Brown had testified it was impossible for him to have left the wheel even for a moment, Captain Humphreys and others had vouched that this was perfectly possible.

"Now why do we discuss Brown? Because, Mr. Foreman and gentlemen, we have followed the accounts of these murders; we have considered the circumstances bearing upon them, and you cannot account for these murders in any other way than that they were the act of a madman—of a maniac. We have looked for a theory; no theory is advanced by the government. . . . He [Hoar] says there was no attempt to ravish Mrs. Nash; there was no assault on her. That element is out. Inquiry was made about the money which Bram had with him. The district attorney now, while he introduced evidence against our objection, which was stated to you by the court—frankness compels the district attorney now . . . to say that he does not attach any importance to the money. That is to say, the indecent assault is out of the question, the money is out of the question. What is the theory? What was a sensible man's motive in committing these murders, in taking these three human lives at that time?

"Has the district attorney suggested any? If he had, what is it, Mr. Foreman and gentlemen? Not robbery, not an indecent assault. What was it? How do you account for it? What else is there to support this theory that this was [other than] the act of a maniac or a madman?"

The court day ended before Cotter could conclude his closing argument, but this he did shortly after court readjourned in the morning. It was January 1, 1897, and Bram, who had to be wondering if he would live to see the new year out, appeared uncharacteristically anxious as Hoar rose to address the jury.

The district attorney promised the jurors that his closing argument would take no more than thirty minutes, and while Hoar actually took an hour, his performance was later praised by the press. Whereas Cotter in his close had mostly focused on Monks and Brown, arguing both had strong motives to shift all suspicion onto Bram, Hoar interpreted select portions of the evidence to implicate Bram in every manner possible.

Hoar pointed out to the jurors (as if they had not been told this countless times before) that, in the hour or so before the murders, only Brown, Loheac, and Bram were topside: Brown at the wheel; Loheac on lookout aft of the forward house; and Bram pacing the deck load amidships, waiting, Hoar argued, for Blomberg to fall asleep below. While Bram waited, he knew that Loheac, who was on lookout forward, could see him but was unaware that Brown, from his vantage point at the wheel, could see him also.

At one thirty, Hoar explained, Loheac briefly left his post and went down into the forward house to fetch his pipe. Believing that the "decks were clean," Bram took that opportunity dash to the afterhouse and once there went "down into the dark and did those deeds. That was his opportunity. He went there."

Erroneously thinking no one had seen him, Bram came back on deck and stuck the ax under a lashing plank on the deck load. But why would Bram hide the ax and not simply throw it overboard?

"Because his deed was not complete," Hoar answered. "Monks was still alive. He [Bram] had got to put that deed on somebody. If the ax was overboard and Monks was aroused from slumber or something like that or Monks was found down there without the ax, that might be something that would not tally with the theory that Monks had done it. That ax had got to be preserved."

However, Bram's intent to "put that game up on Lester Monks or kill him" was foiled when Monks, awoken by the shriek and now armed with a revolver, suddenly appeared at the forward companionway and called for Bram to come below.

Although obliged to follow Monks back into the afterhouse, Hoar explained, Bram was quick to take the swinging lantern from the main cabin and then leave it on the floor of the passenger's cabin. And, Hoar asked, Bram's reason for abandoning the lamp? Because Bram didn't want Monks, when they passed Blomberg's room next to the forward companionway, "to see the second mate laying there."

A "skulking" Bram may well have killed Monks as they exited the afterhouse, except that Monks, who was following behind Bram, had a brand-new revolver that would fire, while Bram had a rusty old one that would not. Once up on the deck load, Bram chose a spot where the ax was hidden from Monks, and then Bram used his time with Monks, between two and four o'clock in the morning, to "think up things." Among the things that Bram thought up, Hoar said, "with the skill and the cunning he has," was the story about Blomberg drugging him and the crew having mutinied.

Hoar said that at daylight, and having stalled as long as he could but still wanting more time "till his mind had got a little clearer and he could arrange himself a little better," Bram went forward to find the steward. If Bram intended this as a ruse to stall longer, however, it didn't work, and "that plucky negro, Spencer," ran into the afterhouse. Before he did this, though, Spencer asked for and was given Bram's revolver. Bram then wanted the passenger's revolver.

"But Mr. Monks had Yankee common sense enough to say that he had better keep that himself; it might come in handy. That was wise."

In terms of the vomit, Hoar explained, Bram stepped into it before a sample could be preserved, which would have put the lie to his claim of having been drugged, and in terms of the ax stuck in the lashing plank, Hoar explained, as he had on the first day of trial, that Bram made sure he saw it first and argued that it must be thrown overboard. That Monks agreed was natural, Hoar reminded the jury, given that Bram had led him to believe the sailors had mutinied.

After the six sailors were questioned and all three bodies were discovered, Hoar said that Bram realized his story about being drugged and about there being a mutiny "would not wash" and changed it to Mrs. Nash having been raped and killed and Captain Nash and Blomberg having killed each other. Then, when that theory "would not wash" either, Bram put the theory on Monks. In the days that followed, Bram did everything he could to be "good natured and friendly" with the crew so as to get them on his side. To confuse the record, Bram had also planned to switch the real log with a doctored log. Finally, Hoar stated that, when Brown was imprisoned in the well in the deck load, Bram had gone to Brown and made the "guilty statement": "Did the passenger tell you that he saw me commit those murders?"

"I say [Bram] did it because Charley Brown says so," Hoar continued, "and I am not afraid to stand on Charley Brown's testimony. I say he did it because circumstances say he did it, because that act speaks louder than any words can speak and says that he did it. No one else had the head to plan. No one else had the thoughts that he wished to put into execution; no one else had the nerve to execute or the cunning to act out that terrible tragedy."

Indicating that he was just about finished with his close, Hoar told the jurors, "I said in the first place that I should not waste any time on compliment. We are all New England people, and we know that we are here to attend each to his own business, according to such light as God has given us, and we do not need either flattery or adulation. I know you are men of business who have come here and been put to the greatest inconvenience to do your duty. I think you will agree that in my opening I did not overstate any of the things I have undertaken to prove and that in my close I have been perfectly fair to the other side in my statement to this case."

Hoar reiterated that Bram could be the only person to have killed the captain, his wife, and the second mate. That Monks could have done it was unthinkable, and as for Brown, explained Hoar, "he had neither the temperament to plan it or the nerve to execute it and act out the part afterwards." Additionally, Brown "as an able or ordinary seaman, would have dared not leave that wheel."

Hoar told the jurors, "If you doubt the character of the witnesses we have produced, murder on the high seas must forever go unpunished because you cannot get any more sensible, honest, clean-appearing fellows than the crew of the *Herbert Fuller* that I have produced here. But, my friends, I am not at all doubtful of the results of this case. I believe in your honesty and in your intelligence, and I believe you will do your duty fearlessly and honestly.

"This is the New Year, which is beginning today. In it, sailors must encounter the god of storms and the demons of the deep, but if this cunning, daring devil goes unpunished by us, then there is to be a new terror added to those who go down in ships unto the sea."

At this, Judge Colt called for a ten-minute recess.

CHAPTER 11

With police in the noisy corridor barking orders to spectators to keep quiet, ten minutes after Hoar's closing, Judge Colt announced that Judge Webb would deliver the charge to the jurors.

Webb commenced his charge, and a reporter for the *Boston Globe* noted, "His honor was visibly affected of the solemnity of the duty imposed on him. He displayed traces of nervousness as he began to speak, and a few moments later when he had occasion to read a definition of murder from a small book, his hands trembled so violently that the fact was apparent to everybody in the courtroom."

Perhaps to control the trembling, the judge thrust his hands deep into his trouser pockets, and with his spectacles thrown high up on his forehead and his silk robe falling gracefully around him, he looked, the reporter wrote, "the picture of benignity and kindness."

His introductory remarks over, Webb then prepared the jurors for the task at hand. Looking directly at the twelve men seated just feet from him, the judge said, "I beg of you, I urge of you, not to start out with the theory that, because the prisoner is an interested party in the proceedings, being the defendant, that therefore his testimony must be rejected. Every man is presumed to be of good character and innocent of crime until the contrary is proved."

Their burden was not to investigate who killed Charles Nash but to solely determine if Thomas Bram killed him, the judge explained. He added that jurors were to carefully weigh Brown's claim that he had witnessed the murder. In particular, jurors were to take into consideration Brown's line of vision as he stood at the wheel; the distance between the wheel and the window looking into the chart room; the height of the window from the deck and the dimensions of the window; and the fact that there had been a ladder in front of the window, bars over the window on the outside, and a curtain that could be drawn shut across the window on the inside.

When the judge had done with his many, many instructions on how the jurors were to evaluate all the evidence, evidence that he painstakingly reviewed for nearly two hours, he concluded his charge with the admonition, "And may he who leads and forms the judgments of men lead you to a righteous and true conclusion upon which your minds and consciences will rest easy during the remainder of your days."

It was now early afternoon, and jurors were escorted to the jury room to begin their work, while Bram, who according to the *Globe* reporter had a "placid smile" that "illuminated his countenance," was removed from the prisoner's dock by Walters and taken down the corridor to the marshal's office. There, Bram could be seen leaning back in a chair, puffing on a cigar, and waiting to learn if he would live or die.

At five o'clock, jury foreman Rinaldo Jack sent word that the jurors were not close to coming to an agreement. The judges gave them more time, and later that evening word spread that the jurors wanted to be read the deposition Brown made for Ingraham in Halifax.

The two judges, along with Hoar and Cotter, had no objection, and so the jurors reappeared in the jury box while Brown's deposition was read aloud. Hours later, when there was still no verdict, the judges ordered deputies McGonagal and Ruhl to take the twelve men back to their room in the Quincy House. With his fate still unknown, Bram was evicted from the marshal's office.

Seeing the defendant go, the *Globe* reporter wrote, "He never walked with a more sprightly step, his mien has not been prouder, his carriage more erect, or his countenance more cheerful than when he was led along the corridors of the Federal Building at 10:30 last night, to be conveyed back to the Charles St. Jail and undergo another night of agony and suspense."

An hour before court was scheduled to reconvene in the morning, the usual riot of would-be spectators was more riotous than usual. They congregated in great numbers at the entrance of the federal building, jamming stairwells and elevators inside the building, and tussled with each other and police in the corridor leading to the courtroom. Despite the melee, on this, the seventeenth day of trial, the crowd, including the usual "ladies of fashion," expected a verdict.

The jurors filed into the courtroom at nine forty, their faces showing the strain of having deliberated for more than twenty-six hours straight (the twelve had continued with their labors at the Quincy House).

Once the jurors were seated, Webb announced that the jury had not reached an agreement and, in a written request, had asked for further instructions. The only instructions he could give them, Webb told the jurors, were the instructions that Sherman Hoar's father, Judge Hoar, had once given a jury: "The only mode, provided by our constitution and laws for deciding questions of fact in criminal cases, is by the verdict of a jury. In a large proportion of cases and, perhaps strictly speaking, in all cases, absolute certainty cannot be attained or expected. . . . You should consider that the case must at some time be decided . . . and there is no reason to suppose that the case will ever be submitted to twelve men more intelligent, more impartial, or more competent to decide it or that more or clearer evidence will be produced. . . . And with this view, it is your duty to decide the case."

The jury was excused to resume its work, and Colt and Webb returned to their lodgings at the Parker House Hotel but not before ordering the marshals to summon them back if needed.

Shortly after twelve noon, they were summoned back. Foreman Jack asked that they be read the testimony given by Loheac and Slice regarding the possibility of Brown being able to look from the wheel down into the chart room.

In a sharp rebuke, however, Webb ruled, "Under no circumstances could the recollection of the court be substituted for the juror's own recollection. . . . You will, therefore, retire for further consideration."

Like everyone else, McGonagal and Ruhl expected the jurors to be done by now and had not planned for their midday dinner, so when word reached the judges at two thirty that the jurors were hungry, the proper victuals were ordered and arrived at the jury room just as the jurors came to a verdict. While the twelve men sat down to eat, the court was informed that a decision had been reached.

The clock in the rear of the courtroom read three thirty, and attorneys, judges, and defendant were once again at their places, waiting for the twelve men to enter. Hoar paced back and forth, a smug smile on his face; one of the Nash brothers watched from a spectator's bench; and Bram, realizing that the momentous hour had come at last, sat in the dock and stared at the floor.

At three forty the jurors appeared in the courtroom doorway, and as they filed past the table where he sat, Cotter tried to scrutinize the face of each man, but each man escaped his gaze by bowing his head. The veteran attorney, the "lynx-eyed counselor," had witnessed many a jury return from deliberations before, and, now certain what the verdict of this jury would be, the lines around Cotter's mouth began to twitch. Sitting next to Cotter at the same table was French, his face pale and drawn.

French leaned forward over the table in anticipation, and when the jury was polled and each responded to his name in barely a whisper, French knew more than he wanted to know. Bram, too, understood that the end had come and, bracing himself for the terrible news, grasped the rail in front of him.

The court clerk ordered, "The jury will stand."

The jurors rose.

"Gentleman of the jury, have you agreed upon your verdict?"

"We have," Jack answered.

The clerk turned to the dock and ordered, "Thomas Bram, raise your right hand."

Bram, releasing his right hand from the rail while still gripping it tightly with his left, did as told. The clerk ordered, "Mr. Foreman, look upon the prisoner; prisoner, look upon the foreman. What say you, Mr. Foreman, is—"

"Guilty."

There was a slight disturbance among the spectators that was instantly quelled by the marshals, and then the clerk had each juror take an oath that guilt was indeed his verdict. All answered yes.

Webb asked Cotter if he wanted to prepare any exceptions before sentencing was pronounced, and Cotter said he did and asked for two weeks. With no objection from Hoar, this was granted. Then Cotter went over to Bram and told his client to be brave.

"If I have got to die, I thank God that I shall die an innocent man," Bram responded, tears running down his cheeks.

His hopes for emancipation dashed, Bram held out his hands to be manacled for the ride back to the Charles Street Jail. His tenure there wouldn't be long, however, because, as legal observers noted, he could expect to hang within months.

Before releasing the jurors, the judges apologized to the twelve for having deprived them of their liberty for so long but assured that each would be immediately taken to Room 112 to receive their jury pay (two dollars per diem, not including the seventy-five cents each had received daily for meals). Exhausted from his efforts and knowing that more work to save his client's life lay directly ahead, Cotter went to his vacation home on Cape Ann for a two-day rest.

The verdict came as a shock, not only to Bram's supporters, who sobbed openly in the spectators' benches, but also to the many attorneys and lawmen who had followed the trial in the newspapers. These critics thought the government's case against Bram exceptionally weak, especially because the government's chief witness, Brown, had been caught falsifying testimony, which for the jurors should have invoked the maxim *False in one thing, false in everything*. The skeptics had predicted that Bram would be exonerated by a finding of not guilty or at least acquitted when the jurors failed to agree either way.

Equally shocking was the manner in which the jurors had come to their decision. It was soon learned that, on the first ballot, a majority, nine to three, was for guilt, and then on proceeding ballots, more jurors joined the majority until, on two successive ballots, only one juror had stood between Bram and death. But then the jurors' sentiments swung in the opposite direction, and at one point those for conviction had shrunk from eleven to seven. More than one hundred votes were taken over twenty hours of deliberations, until finally the exhausted jurors all agreed on guilt.

Little more than a week after the verdict, Cotter went to the Charles Street Jail and informed the wretched man in cell 36 that a motion had been filed with Webb and Colt requesting a new trial.

Cotter was optimistic that a new trial would be granted because of certain things two past clients of his, Abel C. Ford and Harry J. Booth, who also happened to have been jury members, had told him.

Colt and Webb acted quickly and granted a retrial hearing for January 20, a hearing that would prove just as dramatic, acrimonious, and well attended by spectators as the trial itself.

All the main actors from the original drama were there in the courtroom, although, of course, there were no jurors (now enjoying the blessings of freedom) or witnesses (all but Monks and Spencer still languishing in jail). French began by dismissing the verdict as "going against the evidence and the weight thereof" and then denounced the behavior of "one member of the court" and the "tone, language, and manner" of the district attorney's closing argument.

The "one member of the court" was Webb, who, French said, had greatly interfered with the defense's case by constantly interrupting the defense attorneys and their witnesses and by making remarks that the jury could have interpreted as derogatory opinions coming from the bench and directed against the defendant and his counsel. Specifically, said French, Webb had commented that a theory of Cotter's was "far-fetched" and that the loose-leaf notes Bram made from the logbook were, in terms of evidence, "pure manufacture." French then said that Hoar's closing should have been a "calm and deliberate argument" but instead had been a "bitter and personal attack" that relied on passion, prejudice, excluded evidence, and innuendo, such as that Bram's separation from his (in Hoar's words) "wife and three babies—three little children" must have been "for some strong reason" and that Bram (again in Hoar's words) is "evidently of mixed races."

The last comment, French complained, was "belittling the defendant by the insinuation that he was a negro."

Then, armed with the intelligence provided to Cotter by former jurors Ford and Booth, French took a bludgeon to the jury, noting that several members were prejudiced, singling out juror Oliver Briggs in particular. According to French, at one point during the trial, Briggs had said, "There isn't the least doubt but that things are looking bad for Bram, and I believe he is guilty." And then, when Bram was testifying on the stand, Briggs had made a Masonic signal to Bram but received no reply. Afterward, Briggs had told the other jurors, "I am a Freemason. The defendant Bram is not a Freemason; he is a hypocrite." French added that juror Ford, had also prejudged the defendant, admitting that before being empaneled he thought Bram "ought to be hung."

French also revealed that, at ten o'clock on the night of deliberations, the twelve men had conducted a secret experiment in the jury room. The experiment consisted of using the doorway with a window to toilet room 147A to represent the aft wall of the afterhouse and the window looking into the chart room. Jurors used a ruler to mark off a small portion of the toilet-room window to represent the dimensions of chart-room window and some napkins left over from lunch to obscure the rest of the toilet-room window. They put two tables together to represent the elevated afterdeck and lay a cane someone had left in the jury room on top of the tables to indicate the position of the wheel six or seven feet away from the chart-room window. Then the murder was reenacted.

One juror got up on the tables and pretended to be Brown at the wheel, while two other jurors went into the toilet room and shut the door. One of the two jurors, pretending to be Captain Nash sleeping on the cot, sat on the floor, while the other, assuming the role of assailant, stood over him and wielded the ruler as if it were the ax. The fact that the toilet-room window was frosted for privacy did little to deter the jurors from thinking their test a success, and they concluded that Brown could clearly have witnessed the murder.

French argued that, while the experiment "might have influenced, and very probably did influence the opinion of the jurors, . . . it certainly was inaccurate and unsafe and was not a calm and philosophical deliberation on the part of the jury of the proof which had come to them from the witness stand."

French also revealed that, on Friday night during deliberations and when the outside world eagerly awaited a verdict, the jury foreman Rinaldo Jack and juror Booth discovered a piece of paper tucked inside their hats. The paper was from a court bailiff, John "Red" Harrington, and on it was written, "Would you like a ½ pint? If so give me the tip Sat morning. Red."

French added that during deliberations two bailiffs, two waiters, and a physician (even though none of the jurors was unwell) had been allowed into the jury room and had spoken freely with the jurors. And then when the jurors had finally reached their decision but had not yet announced it in court, a marshal and two bailiffs had dined with them in the jury room.

All of these many improprieties, French argued, resulted in a verdict that was "against the law" and that had shaken the foundations of public faith: "It is safe to say that no trial of modern times has attracted more widespread attention; none has caused greater comment; none has aroused more intense feeling; none has been more faithfully and fully recorded by the press than that of the case at the bar. But the fact that almost universal suspicion has attached to the justice of the verdict, that many if not the majority of the public are demanding that it be set aside, . . . [that] is a very strong reason why the discussion and the determination of the question raised by this motion should be characterized by more than ordinary deliberation and by the most painstaking and conscientious examination on the part of counsel and of the court. The question is not now as to the guilt or innocence of Thomas M. Bram. The question raised by the motion is, Was he properly tried? and that is a question in which society and mankind have a far deeper interest."

Bram sat in the dock as French made his plea, and although recently convicted of murder and facing an untimely death, Bram appeared cheerful and had obviously gained some weight. Before the proceedings started, his guards had not prohibited him from saluting those spectators (most of them female) he recognized from the trial or from accepting a box of flowers sent by an admirer.

On the third day of the hearing, Hoar responded to Cotter and French for more than three and a half hours with his typical vigor, stating that "absolute justice was metered out to the defendant" by "twelve men as fair, as honorable, and as just as have ever sat in a jury box."

Hoar said that newspaper reports of the trial were "one-sided," "worthless," and "inadequate" and had turned the public against the prosecution. Hoar accepted the fact that Cotter and French had a "bounden duty to their client to grasp at any straw that may save that drowning man" but pleaded with Colt and Webb to reject the motion for a new trial, stating, "God has given to you two men judgment and conscience, and he meant you to exercise those two qualities in this emergency. Endowed with those gifts, you have been placed in judgment over your fellow men, and if you go outside of those two gifts for the inspiration of your action in this matter, you will, in my humble judgment, not only violate your duty to the defendant and to the community under your oaths, but you will find yourselves depending upon uncertain or partial or irresponsible or partisan men; on hearsay; on rumor; and on everything else on which human judgment should not depend."

At the hearing conclusion five days after its start, Colt and Webb promised that they would rule on the motion without delay. The next day Hoar announced that he "was tired of the job" and would resign as the US district attorney for Massachusetts once the case was settled.

As if not wishing the case to be settled, the *Herbert Fuller* sailed into New York Harbor, fresh from Buenos Aires with a cargo of 67,000 dry hides worth $160,000, and tied up at a Brooklyn pier. Hoar could hardly ignore the arrival of the infamous barkentine, which made front-page news, and so he dutifully informed Cotter that he intended to pay a visit and invited him to come along.

On Saturday, February 6, both men boarded the vessel (Hoar had forbade Cotter to visit alone), and each man conducted his own investigation. Hoar did not divulge his findings, but Cotter, assisted by Spencer, who knew the conditions on that frightful morning, said that, from where he had stood at the wheel, Brown "could not possibly look into the cabin and see the movements of two men placed there to impersonate Captain Nash and his assailant."

Spencer (who all along swore Brown couldn't have seen into the chart room) agreed, and Cotter had Spencer sign an affidavit to this effect. The affidavit, though, did not arrive in Boston in time for Colt and Webb to take it into consideration, and on Tuesday the two judges denied the motion for a new trial.

Bram, in the prisoner's dock, appeared shattered by the decision, and many wondered if he would finally break and confess to the crime.

Fearing the motion would be denied, Cotter and French had taken care to file a supplemental motion the day before, Monday, which contained Spencer's affidavit. The judges reviewed the supplemental motion for several days and then, having called prosecution, defense, and the convict into court yet again, said that Cotter's investigation added nothing the jury had not heard from the carpenter who'd inspected the vessel in Halifax: supplemental motion denied.

Recording the scene, a reporter wrote, "Bram, who had been intently watching the judge while he was reading the decision, now and then wet his lips, while his breast heaved as he listened to the words which destroyed his last hope of another trial, at least as far as this court is concerned."

Bram's last and only hope lay with the highest court in the land, and that hope depended on Colt and Webb allowing the voluminous bill of exceptions Cotter and French had taken during the course of the trial. (In the 1890s, attorneys "took an exception" to formally record their objection to a judge's ruling, such as permitting or not permitting certain testimony or other evidence. Should the attorney then wish to appeal the final verdict to a higher court, these exceptions would form the basis of that appeal.)

There were more than three hundred typewritten pages worth of defense exceptions, and it took Colt and Webb two weeks to sort them all out and decide which, if any, should be allowed. In the end, and against Hoar's vociferous objections, the justices allowed them all. But this was no excuse to delay sentencing, and the only question remaining was if it would be Colt or Webb who would have the unenviable task of telling Bram that he would hang.

A week later the task befell Colt, and prior to reading the sentence, the judge had Bram stand in the dock and answer the simple question, "Have you anything to say why sentence of death should not now be pronounced against you, according to law?"

Responded Bram, "I thank your honor for the opportunity. I now say in the presence of almighty God that I am an absolute innocent man for the crime of which I am charged with. God alone knows that I am innocent. I say now not my will be done but God's will be done on earth as it is done among his angels in heaven."

Ordered Colt, "You will remain standing, Thomas M. Bram. You stand convicted of the murder of Captain Charles I. Nash upon the high seas onboard of the barkentine *Herbert Fuller*."

Before pronouncing sentence, Colt described the crime and the evidence presented at trial in detail, and when done with this, the judge spent time informing Bram, that while he "had the assistance of learned, earnest, skillful counsel" and that while he had received a "fair and impartial trial under the law" before an "upright, intelligent, and patient jury," still he had been found "guilty," which was a "verdict the court sees no just ground of exception."

Then he got to the point: "In this terrible hour of your affliction, and as we approach the sad duty of pronouncing sentence, which is the voice of the law and not our own, we devoutly commend you to the mercy of Almighty God, with whom is abundance of mercy and from whom we may all hope for pardon and mercy. And now nothing remains but the solemn duty of pronouncing the sentence of the law, which is—"

Everyone in the courtroom stood.

"All things having been fully heard and understood by the court, it is considered that the verdict of the jury be confirmed, and you, Thomas M. Bram, be taken back to the place whence you came and there remain in close confinement until Friday, the eighteenth day of June, in the year of our Lord, eighteen hundred and ninety-seven, and on that day, between the hours of eleven o'clock in the forenoon and two o'clock in the afternoon, you, the said Thomas M. Bram, be taken hence to the place of execution and there be hanged by the neck until you are dead, and may God in his infinite goodness have mercy on your soul."

Immediately upon passing sentence and before the condemned man could be taken from the courtroom, Colt directed that the execution be postponed until the Supreme Court had time to consider and respond to Cotter's request for a hearing.

It was March 9, and knowing that the Supreme Court justices went on their respective circuits in May before returning to Washington in October, Cotter and French expected that a hearing, if granted, would likely come in the fall; in due course the two attorneys were informed of just that: the nine justices would hear their case on October 18.

Cotter and French would be allowed just two hours to convince the justices that their client was deserving of a new trial, and senior and junior counsel boarded the morning train to the nation's capital on Friday, October 15, to spend Saturday and Sunday in preparation for court on Monday. News that the high court would hear his case had greatly lifted the spirits of Bram, whose spirits were in need of lifting. According to a reporter who visited Bram in jail, he "has bleached out somewhat during his long confinement and looks paler."

CHAPTER 12

Bram versus United States was heard on Monday afternoon, with French being the first to address the justices. In their brief for the nine men in black robes, French and Cotter listed sixty-seven "different causes of error" during the trial, but the two had only an hour to make their case and so concentrated on only a dozen, principally those they thought were their strongest case for being granted a new trial. French opened for the plaintiff and numerated multiple problems involving jury selection and empaneling, including one juror's having been sworn in after all the others.

Only then did French turn to Halifax detective Power's private meeting with Bram, the one where Bram had been stripped and told that Brown had seen him descend into the afterhouse companionway just before the murders. Argued French, "The whole aim and purpose of the examination and interview was to intimidate the prisoner and induce him to say something which would tend to incriminate him. In the interests of fairness and public justice, such inquisitorial methods should not be countenanced. They are not consistent with the principles of fair play. Testimony of this sort should be admitted with the greatest caution when the prisoner and detective are alone. There must be no direct or implied inducement, however slight, and no exertion of any improper influence."

At the murder trial, French told the nine justices, Power had not only been allowed to testify about his meeting with Bram but also that "one member of the court [Judge Webb] asked the witness leading questions, which are found in the record, to which the defendant objected."

French then dealt with Webb's remark that Bram's loose-leaf notes based on the ship's log were, in terms of evidence, "pure manufacture." Argued French, "If a judge, 'to whose lightest words the jury, properly enough give a great weight,' charges the defendant on the witness stand, in language and effect, with having manufactured evidence to be used to meet an anticipated accusation, the only inference that can be drawn from the remark is, that, in the opinion of the court, the defendant is guilty."

French had other objections as well, concluding with the many "objectionable matters" that had occurred in the jury room during deliberations.

The following afternoon, Cotter reargued all of French's arguments from the day before, including the fact that the jury's impromptu experiment was reason enough to grant a new trial. Then Cotter dramatically told of his own experiment, the one he conducted on the actual *Herbert Fuller*. A British journalist in the courtroom, A. Maurice Low, wrote:

> Every member of the bench sat up straight in his chair and listened intently while Mr. Cotter told the court how, in the early part of February last, the district attorney and himself went to New York, and there had Spencer, the steward, and one of the government's witnesses, arrange the furniture of the cabin precisely in the same shape in which it was at the time when the murders were committed.
>
> He told how Spencer turned the lamp down low, exactly as it was on the fatal night, and how when everything was arranged the district attorney and himself went to the wheel, and holding it with both hands, as Brown alleged he did that night, attempting to look into the cabin, as Brown testified he did, and saw Bram strike the captain.
>
> Neither Dist. Atty. Hoar nor himself was able to see the inside of the cabin from the wheel while holding it with both hands, but when only one hand was on the wheel, and by craning forward, part of the cabin would be indistinctly seen.
>
> Mr. Cotter's recital of this experiment was intensely interesting, and members of the court asked many questions, as to have the whole scene clearly implanted in their minds.
>
> With the description of this scene Mr. Cotter finished his argument, having consumed an hour and a half and having evidently

> raised several very grave doubts in the minds of many members of the court.
>
> A prominent and experienced attorney remarked at [Cotter's] conclusion that he felt certain from the drift in the questions asked by members of the court that a new trial would be granted.

The government was handicapped without the services of Hoar who, of course, knew the case intimately because he had successfully prosecuted it just months before. In the New Englander's absence was Assistant Attorney General James E. Boyd, a former Confederate whose knowledge of the case was secondhand. Boyd ably argued the government's position that no new trial was needed, but he lacked Hoar's legal brilliance and oratorical elegance.

The high court reached its decision in mid-December, and Cotter and French rushed to the Charles Street Jail together to deliver the news in person. The highest court in the land had ruled: "The judgment is reversed, and the cause remanded, with directions to set aside the verdict and to order a new trial."

The justices' reasoning came as a surprise to Cotter and French, who had thought their strongest arguments were those involving the jury. Instead, the high court ruled six to three that Bram's Fifth Amendment right protecting him from being "compelled in any criminal case to be a witness against himself" was violated during his interview with Power. In fact, the majority found "a plainer violation as well of the letter as of the spirit and purpose of the constitutional immunity could scarcely be conceived of."

The date for the second trial was set for March 15 out of consideration for the six witnesses who still languished in the Charles Street Jail (where, for food and miscellaneous expenses each got six dollars a day, or more than they earned onboard the *Herbert Fuller*). Cotter and French represented the accused, and Judge Colt was again captain of the courtroom, with Judge Webb his mate.

A pool of 168 potential jurors had been whittled down to 12 men, who were again all white, and on March 17, the assistant district attorney from the first trial, John H. Casey, delivered the opening argument for the prosecution. Casey took two hours and fifty minutes. When he was done, his boss, the new district attorney, Boyd B. Jones, took over and called the government's first witness, Halifax police sergeant Robert N. Lehan.

The sergeant testified that, on July 21, 1896, he personally untied the defendant from his place on the afterdeck and recalled that Bram had remarked, "To ___ with them; all they can do is to hang me."

Halifax detective Power, having proven fatal to the prosecution's case last time, was not invited to testify again, but Dr. William Finn was, and he again spared no details. (Among them: "One of the wounds had entered the brain substance of Captain Nash to the extent of about four inches, but when I examined the skull of Captain Nash, there was no brain substance; it had disappeared.")

When through with Finn and several other witnesses, including Consul Ingraham, Jones called Lester Monks to the stand.

Appearing, according to a reporter, "far stouter and more rugged" than he did during the first trial, the young man "still has the same slight stoop in the shoulders, however, and his gait has not changed in the interval."

Yet again, Monks told his by-now-familiar tale ("I was awakened by a scream, a shrill scream"), but according to the reporter, "Those who heard Monks testify at the former trial believed he did not display [the] same possession or coolness he did then. He showed more of a disposition to become excited when he was interrupted in his narrative, and he was more flushed and agitated than he was a year ago."

On cross-examination, Cotter caught Monks contradicting several things he had said during the earlier trial, such as now not being sure if he had or had not told Bram of going into Mrs. Nash's room, but overall Monks's story differed hardly at all. After testifying for the better part of an afternoon and then all of the next day, Monks was free to leave the stand forever. (And possibly forever regretting being that callow young fellow of July 14, 1896, who, when awakened by Mrs. Nash's scream, had armed himself with a loaded revolver and, instead of leaping to her aid, had cowered in his stateroom for ten or more minutes.)

Just before the second trial started, the *Herbert Fuller*, under command of a Nash brother, was in Brooklyn, New York, and in the process of unloading a cargo of sugar from Cuba. The barkentine may have escaped the first trial, but it would not escape this one, and under orders from the US government, the tug *Nina* towed it to Boston, where the members of the jury would get their chance to visit the crime scene. First, though, came the testimony of Charley Brown.

Looking, according to a reporter, "more like a prosperous business man than the bedraggled sailor he appeared the day he arrived from Halifax 18 months ago," Brown took the stand. Despite his English, which had improved little since the last trial, Brown made for an effective witness for the prosecution and this time around readily admitted to the shooting incident in Rotterdam. With considerable animation and even some humor, as if the whole thing had been a lark, he told of losing his sweetheart, his money, and his senses in that city and of finally winding up in some institution, where he was told he had, in his words, "shot or shot at" a man.

Presumably, Cotter and French had reached a dead end when it came to learning anything more about the episode because, while Cotter was just as incredulous by Brown's account of the incident as he had been before, he did not drop any new bombshells. Cotter did, though, get Brown to state that once on a train he'd imagined that everyone onboard was about to rob him.

When Brown was excused from the stand on the tenth day of trial, the transcript already ran more than 1,500 typewritten pages, and court observers thought the proceedings might go on for another two weeks.

The other sailors testified, and under cross-examination Slice added a new fact. This was that the door to the after companionway had been open all evening (just as it was when Monks had gone to bed), but when Brown left the wheel at two in the morning, the door had been shut. Also on cross-examination, Andersson said that, when doing a "trick" at the helm, it wasn't always necessary to attend to the wheel, such as when they lashed it while working the kink out of the line to the jolly boat.

Because so much rested for the defense on the point of the wheel being lashed for a prolonged period of time, the prosecution, not to be outdone this time, called a total of thirty-nine ancient mariners to the stand, each testifying that the wheel of a sailing vessel could never be left alone.

While many doubted that the district attorney would ask Spencer to take the stand, given his mercurial performance last time, Spencer was again called to testify for the prosecution. Dressed nattily in a black suit of the latest fashion and wearing a white carnation in his lapel, the witness repeated the various disparaging remarks Bram had made about the captain and his wife but had little more to add except to mention that, on the evening before the murders, he saw Captain Nash drinking liquor in the afterhouse storage room. On cross-examination, however, Cotter wrung a new fact out of Spencer, and this was that Brown not only admitted to pulling down the rod and curtains over the chart-room window but also of closing the aft companionway door.

Among the last government witnesses was Dr. Draper, the coroner who during the earlier trial was deemed unfit by Cotter to speculate on the axing of a human body because Draper had no personal experience in this regard. Since that time, however, the doctor had made up for the deficit and revealed that he had experimented on the body of a woman who died at Boston City Hospital last December. There was a collective gasp in the courtroom. Based on this experiment, the doctor said he could now confirm that it was possible for an ax murderer to avoid being splashed with blood (thus implying that Bram, who by all accounts had no blood on him, could still have been the butcher). Cotter challenged Dr. Draper's testimony, however, when he asked him if he had struck the body on the head.

"Not to penetrate the substance of the skull," the doctor answered.

"On the arms?" asked Cotter.

"No."

"On the chest?" asked Cotter.

"No."

And had he, asked Cotter, struck the neck so as to cut off the head and the arteries?

"No."

Finally, knowing that the three victims had been hacked almost beyond recognition, Cotter wondered, "What was the appearance of the body when you got through with it, Dr. Draper?"

"It looked exactly as it did before I began."

French delivered the opening argument for the defense, and it received high praise from attorneys watching in the spectator benches. Then a number of witnesses of various professions (one was a veterinarian, another a shoemaker) were called to testify. Each had conducted tests aboard the *Herbert Fuller* now that it was in Boston, and all affirmed that to stand at the helm with both hands at the wheel and to look directly into the chart-room window was impossible.

Halifax pilot William Baker took the stand later, swearing that he had been aboard the *Herbert Fuller* when Bram was untied and, contradicting sergeant Lehan, that Bram had never remarked "To ___ with them; all they can do is to hang me." In case anyone doubted it, Baker reached into a pocket and whipped out a knife, saying, "There is the knife with which I cut the rope. Lehan had nothing to do with cutting him loose."

Having endured four weeks of confinement in the jury box, on April 9 the twelve jurors finally got to see the murder scene for themselves. The outing by barge took them to Leighton's Wharf in East Boston, and for one glorious hour the jurors got to tour the *Herbert Fuller*. They even had a chance to stand at the helm and inspect the window looking into the chart room, but they were forbidden from conducting any experiments of their own. Then it was back to the courtroom for an afternoon of hearing more testimony.

The next day, Cotter asked his client to step out of the prisoner's dock.

Bram's being called to testify in his own defense came as no surprise this time, and like other witnesses, his new testimony differed in parts from what he previously said, but almost all was as it had been before.

Impressing court observers with his confidence, the next day Bram ably withstood a merciless, six-hour cross-examination at the hands of the district attorney. When Jones pressed Bram to explain contradictions between his testimony now and his testimony in the last trial, Bram said his earlier testimony must have been correct. When Jones asked Bram what he meant by a certain word or phrase, Bram explained that he had little education and often used language without always understanding its meaning.

Then at one point during the cross-examination, Bram mentioned a subject that in the Boston of 1897 was not to be mentioned. Bram volunteered that he had seen certain evidence that Mrs. Nash had "been interfered with." Not expecting this, Jones had little choice but to inquire what exactly Bram had seen. Hesitating before proceeding in a tone that could only be heard a few feet away, Bram said he was reluctant to because there were a great many women present. Judge Webb, though, would have none of it and declared that, if women went to court, then they must be prepared to hear what was given in evidence. In a louder voice, Bram then related what he had seen, but the Boston newspapers of the day shielded their gentle readers from the facts, and Bram's testimony has been lost to the record.

To the surprise of Jones, when Bram left the stand, Cotter rose to announce that the defense had no more witnesses to call. Jones, however, was not through gathering testimony and, in rebuttal to the argument that it was not possible to both stand at the wheel and look into the window, called more than twenty witnesses to report the findings of their experiments aboard the *Herbert Fuller*, experiments conducted at night and with the help of a man in the chart room pretending to be an ax-wielding assailant.

The moment court opened the next morning, in a quiet voice and reasoned manner, Cotter began his closing arguments, and as before they centered on the guilt of Brown: "I am accustomed to say what I mean and to mean what I say, gentlemen. I shall have occasion to say and I do now say that that man Brown still belongs in some institution and that it is his proper place, whether in a lunatic asylum or in a criminal institution. He is unbalanced, mentally: one of the most cunning of criminals, who ought either be in prison or in a lunatic asylum."

Suggesting that Brown still had something to hide from his time in Rotterdam, Cotter noted, "He has never returned to his own country nor to Holland since his escapade there. He shot a man in Rotterdam, then sat down and smoked a pipe and drank a bottle of beer, and later escaped the penalty of the law by playing insanity.

"Is there, gentlemen upon your panel, a man who would take the life of anybody on the evidence of Brown as you have seen and heard him?

"Brown is the man who, having, according to his own statement, seen Captain Nash killed by Bram, was relieved at the wheel, walked forward, never said a word to the man who relieved him or to anybody in the forecastle, took a bucket from the rack, changed his clothes, and hung them in a most unusual place—beneath the boat."

Again and again Cotter targeted Brown in an indictment lasting exactly six hours. Asked Cotter, "Who pulled down the curtain? Who closed the door into the aftercabin? Charles Brown did it. Charles Brown went into that cabin, where he had no right to be, between the hours of twelve and two o'clock, and [it was] between twelve and two o'clock [when] Captain Nash, his wife, and the second mate were murdered. Charles Brown closed the door, which was none of his duty, and he pulled down the curtain."

But instead of Brown, Cotter argued, "Bram is charged with having intended to kill everybody in that cabin, including Monks. If he did so intend, why did he not do so when he and Monks went below together, when, if the charge against him is correct, he must have known well that there was not a soul alive below to tell about it, and held Monks's revolver while Monks was changing his clothes and made no attempt to kill him?"

At the end of his close and with Bram, who had tears in his eyes, watching from the prisoner's dock, Cotter explained, "My associate and myself have been concerned in this case from the beginning. You have been here for five weeks, away from your homes, your families, and your friends. We have been for two years working on this case. And we are here today, as we were the day the court assigned us to this duty, working because we are officers of that court and working without remuneration.

"Our only reward, the only reward for which we hope, is that, when we are laid away in some remote corner of the country in which we live, people who by our graves will linger long enough to say of us, 'He was faithful to his client, to justice, and to humanity: it made no difference to him what other considerations were when they were assigned to duty by the court, whether a client came from St. Kitts, from Nova Scotia, or our own New England coast or from some other land beyond the sea; duty called them and they performed that duty faithfully.'"

The following day it was the district attorney's final turn to persuade the jury. Appearing pale and haggard from the strain of the trial, which was threatening to break legal records for length, Jones plunged into his closing pleas the moment the clerk declared court open. Jones spoke of the bond that existed between Captain Nash and his wife, of their youthful love in their little seaport village of Harrington, of their hopes to save enough for a quiet retirement on land, and of that last stroll they took together arm in arm on the afterhouse roof "as the shadows were lengthening." But then, in the early morning hours, Jones said, an assailant had reason to kill them.

"It was no insane delirium," Jones said, "that led the man who went down into that aftercabin with catlike tread and first hacked the second mate, then Captain Nash, and finally attacked Mrs. Nash, and dealt her blow after blow until she was dead."

Only three people could have done the crime, Jones stressed: Brown, Monks, or Bram. Of the three, only Bram had a motive, as shown by the disparaging remarks he made about the captain and his wife earlier in the voyage, a motive that, when fueled with alcohol, led Bram to act.

"It was whiskey, whiskey, whiskey, whiskey on his part," insisted Jones, adding that Bram had lied on the stand, for example, claiming to have not known about the ax in the storage room. In contrast to Bram's denial, Jones argued, "Monks, honest boy, no matter what they may say about him—and there has been an attempt to morally assassinate him—Monks says he saw that ax in the storeroom. He was not afraid to admit it, because he had no guilt on his soul. But he [Bram] did not see it. His guilty soul knows that his guilty hands held that ax, and that with his guilty hand, impelled by his guilty heart, with the whiskey he had been drinking intensifying his passions, he took that ax and drove it into the brains of three living human beings."

As for Brown, Jones dismissed the events in Rotterdam as a case of delirium tremens after being at sea for fifteen months and then going on a "seaman's spree" once ashore. Additionally, that episode had occurred years ago and had nothing to do with the crime.

Jones took nearly as long, just under six hours, as did Cotter to make his final case, and while Jones had argued for all the reasons their client should hang, Cotter and French had to give Jones his due and congratulated him for his performance.

Even though the clock read five thirty, Webb and Colt wanted to hurry things along, and Colt delivered brief instructions, just forty minutes, before dismissing the jury to begin its deliberations.

The twelve men, unlike the last twelve, maintained their silence, and so nothing is known about how they arrived at their decision, but at ten thirty the next morning, the foreman informed the court that they had reached a verdict: "Guilty but without capital punishment."

During the fifteen-month interval between the end of the first and the start of the second trial, federal law involving guilt in capital offenses had changed, and jurors could now choose between death or a lifetime of imprisonment. Although Cotter viewed the juror's verdict as a "cowardly" compromise between the noose and freedom when they should have chosen freedom, he dared not press for a third trial knowing that his client had cheated death twice.

That October, Sherman Hoar died a patriot's death at age thirty-eight. The former US congressman and US district attorney had spent the past summer in the southern states with the Massachusetts Volunteer Aid Association, visiting army hospitals for those "boys in brown" from the Bay State who had suffered sickness or wounds as a result of the war with Spain. Hoar saw to it that patients, doctors, and nurses were receiving enough medicine, equipment, and everything else they needed. The work was arduous and the extreme heat of the southern summer insufferable, and Hoar returned home in poor health. Just days before he died, his condition had rapidly worsened. Hoar's peers at the bar were distraught. His brilliant legal career, of which the Bram trial was so far the shining example, had been cruelly cut short, and they now paid tribute to their fallen colleague at a special meeting held in a federal building courtroom.

Sitting in the back row and listening as prominent men rose to give witness to Hoar's life was someone who had every reason to remember Hoar fondly. This was the man who, in the early hours of July 14, 1896, and while in one of his periodic bouts of violent insanity, took an ax and claimed the lives of Charles Nash, Laura Nash, and August Blomberg. It makes no difference if the man's name was Justus Leopold Westerberg; Johese Vastbac; or his latest identity, Charley Brown—the man had still gotten away with murder.

Being a common sailor, Brown was politely ignored, but others in the courtroom that day were not. Among these was Judge Colt, who in a poignant speech remembered of Hoar that "he hated bigotry, cant, and hypocrisy. He was plainspoken and unconventional. His tastes were democratic, and he recognized no distinction in persons. The poor and humble, rich and powerful, were alike to him."

Not to criticize the dead (because, as Bram correctly observed, "the dead cannot speak for themselves"), but perhaps Hoar was not exactly as Colt so charitably remembered him. Perhaps not all people "were alike to him." Perhaps Hoar had recognized "distinction in persons," especially distinctions between men of different races; for instance, a Nordic mariner from Sweden being one type and a "half-bred negro" from Saint Kitts being another. And perhaps in his eagerness to get a conviction in a case that had attracted as much public and press interest as did the *Herbert Fuller* murders, an ambitious man like Hoar, who had stood for public office once before and perhaps intended to do so again, ignored the evidence and decided on a suspect who differed most in appearance compared to the twelve "ordinary" men of the jury and decided on a chief witness who differed the least.

Perhaps.

CHAPTER 13

Today, those vacationing Down East can visit the Forest Hill Cemetery in Harrington just off Route 1 and leave flowers at the graves of the captain and his wife.

In Halifax, however, no flowers can be left at the grave of the second mate because his gravesite, in ground once hallowed for the unclaimed dead, is now covered by streets and buildings. The second mate might have remained unknown to the larger world if not for a little sleuthing on the part of an unnamed *New York Times* reporter, and the second mate's story turned out to be as pathetic as was his senseless murder.

According to the reporter's story for the *Times* on February 7, 1897, August "Bamberg" had been a "hardy, sea-faring young Finlander" whose sweetheart was a "young Finnish maiden, a poor but hard working lass." The reporter explained:

> His parents were poor and his wages, although small, were the best that he would command in that country. He grew restless, and finally decided to leave his sweetheart and his parents and come to America where work was plentiful, men in demand and wages good. He thought, too, that in the course of a few years he might work his way up until the top rung was reached, and he should then command a vessel. When this came he would send for his Finnish sweetheart and they could be married. His parents and sweetheart urged him to return. His parents were getting old and needed the love that a son could give them; but the young fellow's mind was made up and he stayed.

His Finnish name was, the reporter explained, "unpronounceable" in America, so he took a new name.

According to the reporter, the young Finn arrived in New York and found work as a common sailor before, in two years' time, he had made second mate,

> which brought in a little more money.
>
> His letters home continued, but at long intervals. When he returned from a voyage he would write home and enclose the old folks a remittance to keep the wolf away from the door. All this time he was corresponding with his Norse girl.
>
> Last July Bamberg wrote home from Boston that he had secured the berth of second mate on a sailing vessel, the name of which he did not give, and he wrote his sweetheart that he hoped as soon as the voyage was over to be able to command the wages of a mate.
>
> If he succeeded in this he would send for her and they would be married and perhaps bring the old folks to America. This is the last letter his sweetheart and parents have ever received. Weeks grew into months very quickly, but nothing further came from Bamberg to cheer the loneliness of his old home in Finland. Then came rumors, indefinite, but with enough distinctness to cause unease. They said that a murder upon the high seas had been committed and a man, a second mate by the name of Bamberg, had been murdered, together with a captain and his wife.

The victim's parents did not know that their son now went by a different name, but realizing that the murdered mate was Finnish and had sailed from Boston at the very time their son had disappeared, they wrote every Finn they knew in America, begging for information. Then, a Finnish sailor in New York who went by the American name Walter Palmer confirmed their worst fears. The *Times* reporter met with the Finnish sailor at the offices of John Swann on 66 South Street in an attempt to learn the second mate's real name, but according to the reporter, "Mr. Palmer said he could not do it, being unfamiliar with the English language."

Henry J. Slice, like the rest of the sailors, was released from jail in August 1898, even though Bram's second and final conviction had occurred four months earlier. (Fearing that Cotter would argue for a third trial, Jones had insisted that his witnesses stay put for the time being.) After twenty-five months of confinement, Slice found a room with Mr.

and Mrs. George A. Macauley at 24 Chapman Street in Charlestown and gained employment as a porter for the American Express Company. Then one day in September 1901, Slice left work at the usual hour and was never heard from again.

Oscar Andersson used his newfound freedom to study physiology, anatomy, and massage, "with a view," he told a reporter in 1912, "of earning my living by some other means than by following the sea." He worked at Boston City Hospital before becoming manager of the Butler Exercise Club on 306 Washington Street, a position he had held since 1902. In response to the reporter's query, Andersson answered, "I don't know what has become of Charley Brown or the rest of the crew."

And whatever did become of the rest of the crew is still unknown, the fate of Brown, of course, being of greatest interest. The mystery writer Mary Roberts Rinehart investigated the murders for her 1914 novel *The After House*, which was loosely based on the crime, and became convinced of Bram's innocence.

In a newspaper story published in March of that same year, Rinehart said that, while "Bram's conduct was at no time heroic," if he had committed the murders, "he would have undoubtedly have made some attempt to discover if he had any incriminating stains. He did not. He sat on the roof of the after house with the passenger until daylight." Rinehart also said that Bram, "seeing the passenger, wild eyed, in his night clothes running toward him," had every right to have "grabbed a plank, who wouldn't?" Then, in 1931, Rinehart wrote in her memoir *My Story* that she had since come "into possession of information that the Scandinavian nicknamed Charlie Jones [*sic*] by the crew, had some years after the murders been taken with a sudden attack of homicidal mania in a hospital in Stockholm, and had tried to kill his nurse with a knife."

Monks went on to lead a private life, the barest facts of which can be gleaned from a brief article appearing in the *Boston Daily Globe* on September 2, 1911; an alumnus note he wrote for Harvard in 1913; and his obituary of September 27, 1927.

The brief article states, "Mrs. Frances F. L. Monks, wife of Lester H. Monks," had filed for divorce in Dedham civil court on the grounds of "cruel and abusive treatment . . . that existed through a long and continuous period up to March, 1910, when on account of this treatment, she was obliged to leave him. She asks for the custody of two children." The article notes that the couple was married on May 10, 1900, in Washington, DC, "and the ceremony at the church of the Covenant was a fashionable one."

Although Monks quit Harvard before graduating with the class of 1898 (but always took care to list himself as "H '98" in the *Social Register*), his classmates asked him to submit a note for their *Quindecennial Report*. And although the 415 "warriors of '98" (as the class called itself) obviously knew of his ill-fated voyage aboard the *Herbert Fuller* (Bram's trials, extensively covered by the newspapers, occurred during their last two years of college), Monks chose to ignore this fact. Instead, as if he had never intended to go to Argentina and had never found himself in mortal fear for his life hundreds of miles out to sea and had never worried about being accused of triple murder upon reaching shore, Monks implied that he had spent the summer of 1896 in mundane employment. The entirety of his note for the report reads:

> Became office boy for Philadelphia and Reading Coal and Iron Company in May, 1896; in December the same year I decided bituminous coal offered more opportunity than anthracite, consequently secured a position as salesman for Morrisdale Coal Company. In 1902 Warren and Monks Company, coals, was formed. I have been its treasurer since. Our business is altogether wholesale.

The obituary (whose heading Monks would not have appreciated: "H. L. Monks' Death Recalls Sea Crime") naturally starts with the deceased's connection to the murders and then incorrectly states (but Monks would have appreciated) that "in the midst of the excitement of the trials" he "was attending Harvard, getting his degree in 1898." The obituary omits mention of his wife having left him but does say that, in 1911, the year she filed for divorce, he gave up much of his coal business and departed for British Columbia, before returning east in 1915, when he married again. Then, according to the obituary, Monks heard the calling of the ocean again, only this time in a strictly financial sense. He entered the shipping business and, maintaining offices on Congress Street in Boston and Wall Street in New York, over the years acquired substantial interests and assumed important positions in the Shawmut Steamship Company, the Marine Investments Company, the American Hawaiian Transportation Company, and several other maritime firms.

Perhaps still searching for adventure but of the safer sort, during World War I he joined the Plattsburg Movement, in which wealthy men like him, too old to enlist, attended army training camps at their own expense. At age fifty-one, Monks unexpectedly died of heart failure in his home on Beacon Hill.

The *Herbert Fuller* continued on as before, its sleek bow parting the deep waters ahead and, year after year, returning a reliable profit to its twenty-nine owners. These included John Swann and members of the Nash and Ray families, plus numerous other individuals, among them someone named Herbert Fuller, presumably the vessel's namesake. The barkentine was not only a testament to the shipbuilding skills of Alonso Nash but also to the viability of the sailing ship in the age of steam. To get to where it was headed, a steamer required expensive oil or coal and also men of mechanical training and experience, men who had to be well treated, well paid, and whom the captain, knowing they were difficult to replace, could not discharge at his earliest convenience. In contrast, to get to where it was going, a vessel like the *Herbert Fuller* wanted little more than a gust of wind and a half-dozen souls resigned to the hard life, low wages, and uncertain future of an ordinary sailor.

The *Herbert Fuller* in its time had, of course, seen death by design but also its share of storms and groundings, although it had never seen that scourge of the wooden vessel: fire. That is until 1916. While tied up at a lumberyard in Port Tampa, Florida, somehow the barkentine became alight. By the time the conflagration had been extinguished, its sides and deck were scorched, its spares and rigging burned, and its forward house completely gutted. Damage, Swann informed the other owners by letter, was "conservatively" estimated at $7,000, but the Boston Insurance Co. would pay just $2,100. Swann asked, Did they want to repair the vessel at cost or "sell to the highest bidder?"

Nineteen of the owners responded to the query, and their unanimous decision was in favor of the latter. Negotiations for the transfer of ownership were completed on April 25, 1916, when a man named E. Lutz of Pensacola, Florida, bought the *Herbert Fuller* for $35,000. Lutz repaired the vessel, converted it to a schooner (which involved rerigging the sails on the foremost mast in the fore-and-aft manner), and renamed it the *Margaret B. Rouss*. Within a year, Lutz's investment had gone to the bottom of the ocean. From the May 30, 1917, edition of the *New York Times*:

> *SANK AMERICAN SHIP AND ROBBED THE CREW*
> *Germans Searched the Captain and Sailors of the Schooner Rouss after They Took to Boats*
>
> Captain Frederick L. Foote of the American schooner *Margaret B. Rouss* arrived yesterday at an American port with seven members of the crew of his vessel, which was torpedoed without warning on April 27 about forty-five miles off the coast of Monaco, on the Riviera. Captain Foote brought the first news of the sinking of the vessel. He said the crew of the German submarine behaved like pirates of the olden days and robbed him and his crew of every article they possessed when they were in the lifeboat.
>
> "We left St. Andrew's Bay, Fla., on Feb. 4 for Genoa with a cargo of pitch pine. All went well until just after 6 o'clock on the evening of April 27, when the schooner was about forty-five miles off Monte Carlo. Suddenly a torpedo struck the vessel on the starboard side amidships with terrific force and tore her planks open. We got the lifeboat launched safely, and had just clambered into it with what articles could easily be saved when a submarine appeared on the surface about half a mile away to starboard. A boat put off from her side with the commander, a junior officer, and four seamen, and pulled over to the *Margaret B. Rouss*, which did not sink quickly on account of being laden with lumber.
>
> "After ordering me to stand by with the boat, the commander and his party went on board the schooner, where they spent two hours rummaging the cabins and storeroom, and filled their craft with all kinds of loot. Not content with that, the Germans came alongside our boat, and the sailors searched our clothes and took away everything we had, including money, tobacco, pipes, and food. They also carried away my sextant, compass, charts, and the ship's chronometer. They pulled back to the schooner, which was not sinking fast enough to please the commander, and put bombs in her hold which blew her up.
>
> "After pulling for forty-five miles over a calm sea, we landed at the port of Monaco, and climbed up to Monte Carlo, where James Gordon Bennett and the Prince of Monaco took care of us and sent us home."
>
> The *Margaret B. Rouss* formerly was the *Herbert Fuller*, which was the scene of a marine tragedy in July, 1896, when Captain Nash,

> his wife, and the second mate, Bloomberg [*sic*], were killed in their berths by Thomas Bram, the first mate. Bram was convicted in Boston and sentenced to life imprisonment.

After his second conviction in 1898, Bram was transferred from the Charles Street Jail to the Charlestown State Prison, a short distance away, to serve out his sentence. Then, however, the brand-new federal penitentiary in Atlanta, Georgia, announced that it had three thousand vacancies to fill. The prison in Charlestown responded to the call by selecting John Davis (head of the Revere gang of counterfeiters), Dr. Robert Thompson and Edward B. Wiggin (associates in counterfeiting), and Louis Berkowitz and Morris Levenson (also counterfeiters) for the trip south. The Charlestown prison also saw fit to select James F. Black and Frank Webb (who robbed post offices for a living) and Thomas M. Bram (of the "Bram case") for the same journey.

None of these men wanted to go. "I am satisfied here—as satisfied as any man can be who is serving a life sentence for a crime he is not guilty," said Bram. "Here I have good food, kind treatment, the companionship of men I know, work enough to keep my mind off my troubles during at least part of the time, and under all circumstances I have a true and loyal friend in Warden Bridges."

As with anything to do with Bram, the public learned of when and where he would be sighted, and sure enough, when the Charlestown deportees arrived at South Station at eight o'clock in the evening of November 26, 1906, to board a special, heavily guarded train, a surging mob was on hand to greet them.

Noted a reporter who managed to squeeze through, "The prisoners were clothed in civilian attire, with overcoats, and they all bore the unmistakable pallor, except Bram, who looked more like a dark skinned Portuguese. He has grown a full beard, streaked with gray." Two days later word reached Boston that the convicts had arrived in Atlanta.

The US Constitution, Article II, Section 2, Clause 1, states that the president "shall have Power to grant Reprieves and Pardons for Offenses against the United States, except in Cases of Impeachment," and with the help of his old counsel, James E. Cotter, who had never forgotten him, on December 29, 1911, Bram formally petitioned President William Howard Taft for a pardon.

Per routine, Bram's petition was sent not directly to Taft but to the US Department of Justice in Washington, DC. Also as per routine, the department sent it to the US district attorney's office that originally prosecuted the crime, requesting a favorable or unfavorable report.

The district attorney for Massachusetts was none other than Asa P. French, appointed to the job by President Theodore Roosevelt in 1906. Although French refused to release a copy of the report he sent back to Washington, he did say that it was "favorable."

French cautioned, however, that his report was one of several things the department of justice would take into consideration before deciding whether to pass the petition along to Roosevelt's successor, William Taft.

The following year, September 1912, it was learned by the press that officials in Washington thought Bram's case to be an extremely difficult one and that it would puzzle Taft. Instead of delivering it to the president, the officials had decided to let the petition sit on a desk and see if, during its next session, Congress acted on changes to the parole law, changes that would grant parole to federal prisoners who had served at least fifteen years of their sentences.

The law was changed, and on August 27, 1913, after seventeen years of imprisonment, including a half-dozen in Atlanta, where, according to the penitentiary warden, William H. Moyer, "he has been a great force for good," Bram was told he was free to go.

Asked what his plans were, Bram said, "The first thing I am going to do is buy is a bunch of flowers; and I'm going to send them to Warden Moyer. He has been kind to me. Then I am going to get a room and go into it by myself and have a good cry. I've got to have that cry before I can realize it's true. Then I'll want to pray a little. And after that I want to work."

Atlanta is a landlocked city, and Bram, who presumably had to remain close to the penitentiary as a condition of parole, went back to the only profession on land he knew: restaurants. Lacking the means to open a proper establishment, he settled for a hot dog stand in the Inman rail yard while also working nights for the Southern Railway as a weight master at a salary of fifty dollars a month. In time, Bram had sufficient money to move his hot dog stand to a more desirable location on Marietta Street, near Broad.

Never one for slack, Bram kept his night job, but the stigma of being a convict prevented him from moving up. In writing President Woodrow Wilson on October 7, 1915, Bram asked for a full pardon "because being a prisoner is a decided handicap to my business progress, and does block my promotion to better paying positions."

A supporting letter from his boss, J. W. Whittaker, general yardmaster, confirmed that Bram's being a convict prevented him from a promotion. Whittaker added that, while he knew nothing about the offense the man had been convicted of, "he is one of the best workers I have ever saw."

Cotter and French certainly lobbied Wilson for a full pardon (Bram thanked them in a letter dated July 30, 1921), but the main force was intervention by US Senator Thomas W. Hardwick of Georgia, opponent of the Ku Klux Klan and champion of prison reform, which included the banning of flogging. Although there's nothing in the Wilson presidential papers regarding Bram, from Versailles, where he was engaged in the peace conference that ended the First World War, the president did telegram a pardon to Atlanta in April 1919.

After six years of toil and self-denial, Bram had saved enough money to purchase the Bromwell apartments in Atlanta on North Boulevard near Highland Avenue and later joined the Florida land rush by transferring his activities to Jacksonville. But none of this compensated for the consuming ambition of his life, and so in 1926, he partnered with the Roseland Corporation of Jacksonville to become the master and managing owner of the schooner *Alvena*.

The single-deck *Alvena* measured 186.6 feet in length, 39.7 feet in breadth, and 14.3 feet in depth. Weighing 772 gross tons, the vessel had four masts and, manned by a crew of seven, could carry slightly under one million feet of board lumber or ten thousand tons of coal. Built in 1901 in Fairhaven, California, before coming east, the *Alvena* had profitably plied the Pacific lumber and copra trade, earning its building costs several times over.

By the time it ended up in the hands of the Roseland Corporation and Captain Bram, however, the vessel was practically a derelict. Its hull leaked, its sails were old and a few of them rotten, and the rigging was so far gone that when parted it was beyond repair.

Undeterred, Bram put his new charge at work in the hard-pine trade between Florida and New England, but rates were low, especially during the Depression years. As the maritime writer Francis E. Bowker (who sailed on the *Alvena* but after Bram's time) explained, "There wasn't much left over for new sails and rigging after expenses were paid. Several times she was towed in with torn sails and insufficient provisions."

Some of these incidents earned Captain Bram national headlines, the first being in early January 1928, when Bram and his men set sail from Jacksonville for Portland, Maine, with a load of lumber. Beset by heavy seas and thick snow off Cape Hatteras, Bram requested that a passing steamer, the *Sixaola*, radio Norfolk that his main and auxiliary pumps were disabled. Hearing the message of distress, the Coast Guard searched the area, but no trace of the famous captain or his schooner could be found.

The nation's newspapers reported the loss but not without a note of irony, pointing out that Bram had twice escaped death for the killings aboard the *Herbert Fuller*, only to be consumed by the sea. A week after his obituary appeared, Bram and the *Alvena* sailed into Portland Harbor. Perhaps a little embarrassed, the captain explained that his message regarding the pumps had been a "precautionary measure" and not a call for help.

During another stormy winter four years later, in 1932, Bram again set forth from Jacksonville with a load of lumber, only this time bound for New London, Connecticut. Ten days after that, the *Alvena*, flying distress signals and with its flooded decks threatening to slip below the waves at any moment, was sighted thirty miles south of the Fire Island lightship. The Coast Guard destroyer *Abel P. Upshur* rushed to the scene. There, Captain Bram explained he had been caught in a gale and snowstorm the previous night. He accepted a tow from the destroyer and, with his crew working the pumps to keep the *Alvena* afloat, arrived safely at harbor.

Next time, it was the Coast Guard cutter *Algonquin*'s turn to rescue the *Alvena*. Once again making a winter run with lumber from Jacksonville to Portland one night in December 1934, the schooner, its sails torn to shreds, was seen flying distress signals off the Pollock Rip lightship by passing vessels. When the *Algonquin* reached the *Alvena*, it was seventy miles from Provincetown, Massachusetts. Captain Bram accepted a tow to Truro, but the line broke in the heavy swells. Bram anchored for the night, and the next morning the tow to safety resumed.

On January 24, 1936, it was the Coast Guard cable boat *Pequot*'s chance to rescue Bram. Again, the cargo was lumber, and arriving from Jacksonville and seven miles from Portland Harbor, the *Alvena*'s mate, Henry Williams, set a course four points off the lee of the Portland lightship in order to pass at a safe distance. Then, however, a gale caused the schooner to drift. Looking up, Williams saw the red-painted hull of the lightship dead ahead and ordered the helm swung hard down. The *Alvena* took the impact amidships, as it raked across the lightship's bow. Both vessels suffered damage, although the *Alvena* fared worst. The lightship remained at its station, while Bram hove to at Halfway Rock before the *Pequot* towed him to Portland. Commenting on his much-battered vessel, which now had a four-foot gash in its starboard side, Bram told a reporter, "She's like me, hard to sink."

The four-master from the Pacific was not only hard to sink but also had unusually fine lines, which made it faster than most of its East Coast brethren. In April 1928, Bram shattered a record of twenty years standing when the *Alvena* rattled down from Jacksonville to Portland in just eight and a half days. The next January, Bram had again made excellent time, beating several other captains to be the first one into Portland Harbor bearing lumber from Florida that year. While berthed at Brown's Wharf on Commercial Street, Bram learned from a newspaper account that his trunk from the *Herbert Fuller* had been found in the Post Office Building in Boston, where, now covered in a thick layer of dust, it had been stored for thirty-two years behind barred and locked doors. The grand old building and its federal courtrooms, in which Bram had twice stood trial, was slated for demolition, and Bram immediately telephoned Chief Deputy US Marshal James A. Tingle and said he wanted the trunk saved and would retrieve it that week. (The trunk, violated so often before by those seeking to connect Bram to the murders, was violated one last time when reporters learned of its existence. The reporters opened the trunk, and inside they discovered only a Bible with Bram's favorite passages marked; books, including one on navigation and others of the religious type; some dusty, moth-eaten clothing; a match safe; a stick of chewing gum; and a sea captain's hat.)

Before Bram left for Boston to fetch his trunk, a reporter went aboard the *Alvena* and found Bram's men, who spoke well of their captain, "dining on roast chicken in the galley, a delicacy not served on every lumber boat." Continuing, the reporter wrote, "Capt Bram was reticent to interviewers. To a reporter, he said: 'I am innocent and always have been, and have tried to live an honest life.'"

What was going through Bram's mind as, now a free man, he approached the Post Office Building? We will never know. But once inside, Bram was all business, going straight to the marshal's office and retrieving what was rightfully his. There was, naturally, a crowd waiting, including newspaper reporters. Bram, though, refused to have his picture taken, saying he wanted no publicity but only wished to be left alone and go his way in peace and quiet.

The 1936 incident in Portland almost a decade later turned out to be a costly one, and it would end Bram's seagoing days forever. Damage to the *Alvena* was estimated by Bram to be $4,000, and in addition to this expense, the schooner was held liable for harm caused to the lightship. This was money that Bram and the Roseland Corporation did not have, and so the US Marshals Service seized the *Alvena* and auctioned it off for a mere $1,850.

According to the US census of 1940, Bram was again living in Brooklyn, New York, and married to a Harriet Bram. He told the census worker that he was "white" and from the "British Isles" and that he rented his home and labored in a warehouse for forty-eight hours a week at $6,600 per year. In 1945, and now age eighty-one, Bram was still married but had moved back to Jacksonville, Florida. He then moved to another place from his past, Georgia, where he was last seen in 1952 walking out of a house with all his worldly possessions, an old mariner adrift.

BIBLIOGRAPHY

"Atlanta Career Recalled as Sea Captain Vanishes." *Atlanta Constitution*, January 11, 1928.

Boston Athenæum. Collection relating to the Bram trial.

Boston Daily Globe.

Boston Evening Transcript.

Boston Herald.

Bowker, Francis E. *Blue Water Coaster*. Camden, ME: International Marine Publishing, 1972.

Bram v. United States. 340 (1897).

Bunting, W. H. *Portrait of a Port: Boston, 1852–1914*. Cambridge, MA: Harvard University Press, 1971.

Evening Mail (Halifax, Nova Scotia).

Goddard, Thomas P. I., and Caroline Hazard Goddard. *Fly Rails and Flying Jibs: Coasting Schooner Photographs by Robert H. I. Goddard*. Mystic, CT: Mystic Seaport Museum, 2011.

Gordon, Bob. "The Strange Career of Detective Nic Power." *Halifax Magazine*, September 25, 2015.

Grinnell, Charles E. "Why Thomas Bram Was Found Guilty." *Green Bag*, April 1897.

Halifax Herald.

Halifax Morning Chronicle.

Harvard College Class of 1898. *Quindecennial Report*. June 1913.

Harvard Law School Library. Thomas Bram manuscript (HLS MS 4086).

Harvard University Archives. Lester Hawthorne Monks student record card (UAV 513.234, Box 3).

Howell, Douglas E. "The *Saladin* Trial: A Last Hurrah for Admiralty Sessions." *Northern Mariner/Le Marin du nord* V, no. 4 (October 1995): 1–18.

Lloyd's Register of British and Foreign Shipping. 1892.

Longfellow, Henry Wadsworth. "Michael Angelo: A Fragment Dedication." *Complete Poetical Works of Henry Wadsworth Longfellow*. Boston: Houghton Mifflin, 1940.

Lubbock, Basil. *The Down Easters: American Deep-Water Sailing Ships, 1869–1929*. Boston: Charles E. Lauriat, 1929.

"Murder Mystery of the Sea." *Day*, May 9, 1960.

New York Times.

Parker, W. J. Lewis. *The Great Coal Schooners of New England, 1870–1909*. Mystic, CT: Marine Historical Association, 1948.

Pearson, Edmund Lester. *Studies in Murder*. New York: Macmillan, 1924.

Portland Press.

Raddall, Thomas H. *Footsteps on Old Floors: True Tales of Mystery*. Garden City, NY: Doubleday, 1968.

Rinehart, Mary Roberts. "Mary Roberts Rinehart Believes That Bram Was Not Guilty of Murders: Attempt to Right a Wrong." *Boston Daily Globe*, March 22, 1914.

———. *My Story*. New York: Farrar & Rinehart, 1931.

Russell, William Clark. *A Voyage to the Cape*. London: Chatto & Windus, 1888.

Sager, Eric W. *Seafaring Labour: The Merchant Marine of Atlantic Canada, 1820–1914*. Montreal: McGill-Queen's University Press, 1989.

South Street Seaport Museum, New York, NY. Barkentine *Herbert Fuller* Collection, 1890–1916.

Sweetser, M. F. *King's Handbook of Boston Harbor*. Cambridge, MA: Moses King, 1882.

Whitaker, Jan. "Dennett's." *Restaurant-ing through History* (blog). August 12, 2013. http://restaurant-ingthroughhistory.com.

INDEX